W9-BFW-646

American Mosaic

American
Mosaic

AFRICAN-AMERICAN CONTRIBUTIONS

African Americans in Film and Television

Cookie Lommel

CHELSEA HOUSE
PUBLISHERS
A Haights Cross Communications Company

Philadelphia

Frontis: Will Smith and wife Jada Pinkett with their children. Smith is now one of the entertainment industry's most recognizable superstars whose career reached an all-time high with his Oscar nomination for his role in *Ali* in 2002, alongside nominations for fellow African-American actors Denzel Washington and Halle Berry.

CHELSEA HOUSE PUBLISHERS

VP, New Product Development Sally Cheney
Director of Production Kim Shinners
Creative Manager Takeshi Takahashi
Manufacturing Manager Diann Grasse

Staff for AFRICAN AMERICANS IN FILM AND TELEVISION

Associate Editor Benjamin Xavier Kim
Production Editor Jaimie Winkler
Picture Researcher Pat Holl
Cover and Series Designer Keith Trego
Layout 21st Century Publishing and Communications, Inc.

A Haights Cross Communications ✦ Company

http://www.chelseahouse.com

First Printing

1 3 5 7 9 8 6 4 2

Library of Congress Cataloging-in-Publication Data

Lommel, Cookie.
   African Americans in film and television/Cookie Lommel.
      p. cm. — (American mosaic)
Includes index.
   ISBN 0-7910-7268-1 (hardcover) — ISBN 0-7910-7491-9 (pbk.)
   1. African Americans in motion pictures. 2. African Americans
on television. I. Title. II. Series.
PN1995.9.N4 L66 2003
791.43'089'96073 — dc21

                                               2002154354

Table of Contents

Comedian Eddie Murphy was one of the first major African-American superstars in film to command a major salary per picture ever since his 1982 movie *48 Hrs.* He is still a consistent box-office draw even today, as evidenced by the success of his *Nutty Professor* and *Dr. Dolittle* movies.

Origins of
an Image

The blockbuster movies and television shows of the new millenium showcase the talents of African Americans in major roles: *Scary Movie*, directed by Keenan Ivory Wayans, grossed $42.3 million in its first weekend, breaking records for an R-rated movie. Martin Lawrence's *Big Momma's House* earned $113 million. And Eddie Murphy's *Nutty Professor II: The Klumps* debuted at number one at the box office.

In 2002, the Academy Award nominations also reflected an exciting change. It was the first time in history that two African-American males had been nominated for Best Actor, with Will Smith (for his role in *Ali*) and Denzel Washington (for his role in *Training Day*) both vying for this coveted award. And Halle Berry, the first black actress nominated since Angela Bassett in 1993, was in the running in the Best Actress category for *Monster's Ball*.

Ask any American who Laurence Fishburne, Wesley Snipes, Danny

Glover, Samuel L. Jackson or Morgan Freeman are. Chances are that they will know them to be great actors—great African-American actors, whose work carries films and whose faces decorate magazine covers. But when you examine how much money these actors earn, none of these African Americans earns the same salary per picture as Tom Cruise, John Travolta or Harrison Ford.

But what do Martin Lawrence, Eddie Murphy, Will Smith and Chris Tucker have in common? In a profession dominated by white actors, film directors and screenwriters, white cameramen and sound technicians, all four of these African-American megastars earn more than $20 million per movie. But they have something else in common—something profoundly influenced by the image of African Americans as entertainers since the minstrel shows of the nineteenth century. All four are comic actors. They're also all male. As African-American film historian Donald Bogle notes, "There is no African American woman who has real box office clout." Halle Berry is paid about $2.5 million per film—not a small amount until it is compared to Julia Roberts' salary of $20 million per film, or to that of a male colleague.

There is a question American film audiences should be asking themselves. Since African Americans make up thirteen percent of the population and twenty-five percent of all movie goers, and most movie tickets are sold to color-blind eighteen to twenty-four-year olds, why are African Americans paid, and represented, so infrequently and so stereotypically on television and in films?

The answer is buried deeply in American history. After the United States defeated Great Britain for a second time in the War of 1812, historian Robert C. Toll observed that "Many Americans expressed the need for native forms, symbols, and institutions that would assert the nation's cultural distinctiveness as clearly and emphatically as the war had reaffirmed its political independence." Simply put, Americans wanted to carve out their own lifestyle, not merely reflect their European origins. And a significant cultural factor in early nineteenth America was the widespread institution of slavery. Slavery had a profound impact on the development of genuinely American forms of entertainment. Attitudes towards African Americans fostered by slavery even now influence big and small screen entertainment.

The most important factor in the development of American theater forms was the rejection of what was seen as European snobbishness. America, which had thrown off the dictates of a European king, wanted the common man of American democracy glorified. On stage, Americans did not want to see kings and aristocrats and perfect gentlemen. They wanted to see a folk culture which mirrored the values of their newly emerging nation. Not all of those values reflected genuine equality, however. The African American was still not a citizen in the country that reaped his labor.

But the African-American presence was not ignored either. Black America made up a significant percentage of the population, and the varying folk cultures, which came with slaves from Africa, were rich in songs, storytelling, and jokes. These forced immigrants, however, were cut off from their own family and specific cultural units, and began to forge a new group identity, according to Toll. The result of this interaction between slaves and owners was a form of entertainment which provided some benefits to both groups: the minstrel show.

City-dwelling audiences primarily desired to be seen as "just folks." They delighted in presentations of joke-cracking, dialect-speaking stage characters which they fondly imagined populated the rural areas, just as Europeans centuries earlier had delighted in the depiction of tranquil farm life. Americans, hungry for a national identity which above all rejected the anti-democratic principles of Europe, wanted the man on stage to be an "Everyman" drawn from even the lowest of social ranks. And slaves were on the bottom of that heap.

Black characters—often white men with their faces painted black, known as "blackface"—rose in popularity. Urban stage audiences in the North, unaccustomed to seeing blacks daily, accepted this caricature of an African American and took it to heart. They shuffled comically across the stage, posing no threat to their masters or to Northerners who fondly imagined that they had fewer racial prejudices than their white Southern brethren had. They sang, they danced, and they soothed a nation's conscience.

One of the first minstrel shows recorded was in February of 1843, when a group of four white Virginia men smeared their faces with burnt cork and pretended to be African Americans. They performed in a small dance hall in New York City, and enjoyed such popularity that more shows were immediately created.

One of the earliest performers was Thomas Dartmouth Rice, who was also known as "Daddy" Rice. He said he was inspired by an elderly black man in Louisiana singing a song about Jim Crow that went, "Weel about and turn about and do jis so,/ Eb'ry time I weel about I jump Jim Crow." The phrase "Jim Crow" was seized upon, eventually occupying an infamous place in American history that became synonymous with institutionalized racism. Rice himself enjoyed such success with his act that he took his show on the road to New York City.

Entrepreneurs like P. T. Barnum seized hold of the enormous potential market for blackface theater and tailored his stage characters to match what his audience demanded. And genuine black performers actually joined these minstrel shows, some drawn by the freedom and money it offered even as the image of African Americans was often degraded by it. Minstrelsy reinforced the stereotypes that many Americans knew and wanted, particularly as the nation was drawn into ever deepening controversy about the role of slavery in the United States.

Americans wanted blacks to be the "other"—to be exotic and different, in order to justify the exploitation of a large group of

White actors Charles Mack and George Moran were just a few of the many white actors who performed in blackface, presenting a safe—yet grossly exaggerated and demeaning—portrayal of African Americans in traveling minstrel shows and films, for the entertainment of white audiences.

human beings. Therefore performances which stressed the African roots of the minstrels were wildly popular. Performers were called upon to do the "Nubian Jungle Dance," the "Congo Melody," or the "African Fling," and were expected to talk in outrageously exaggerated dialects. If the show looked different enough from the average white performance, it was easier to believe that it was "authentic," Toll notes.

The other desire of the average American theatergoer was for the performance to be sanitized. In other words, no matter how romantically savage the black performer was, the audience could relax and feel safe from the considerable violence they relished watching. Therefore, the African-American character depicted would have a comical bent. The minstrels would roll their eyes and stage pratfalls and misunderstand speech; they would seem to be enjoying themselves performing for the white-by-law and by tradition audiences, no matter how ridiculous the material.

The presentations of black culture and physical attributes were frequently grotesque. Blacks did not have hair, supposedly; it was referred to as "wool," like an animal's. Some minstrel shows claimed that blacks filed their hair instead of cutting it. Their lips were exaggerated, their noses flattened, their eyeballs bulged out, and all they wanted, audiences were told, was to eat "possum" and "coon."

Moreover, these characters alleviated guilt over slavery. Minstrel performers frolicked gleefully on stage, singing songs like "The Happy Darky." A popular image of the South perpetuated by minstrel characters was that of the kind master giving slaves their freedom, only to have it refused by the slave so that he could remain a grateful servant in his plantation home, content and loyal. When the Civil War erupted, minstrels even parodied black soldiers for the North as silly dandies in uniform who did their colored kin a disservice by wanting to set them free.

The image of an African American as a pet and a child who needed paternal oversight disguised the very real fear that Americans had of financially independent black citizens. Billy Birch even suggested that "money am de ruination of all de colored folks," to justify keeping them from the fruits of their labors. And a minstrel asked the question America itself worried over, "Now if dey set de negroes free, whar is dey gwine to send them?"

Americans in the '80s who were watching sitcoms like *Diff'rent Strokes* or *Webster*, where an extraordinarily tiny African American plays a child with a white guardian, should have heard alarms ringing as the minstrel show replayed itself across their televisions. African Americans are making inroads into a less bigoted realm of self-expression and crafting film and television releases with more dignity and authenticity, such as the highly successful program *The Cosby Show*. Yet *Webster*, just like the minstrel shows of yore, proved to be so wildly popular that its formula will surely persist on-screen, just as they have influenced the entire history of African-American film.

Actor Louise Beavers was one of the most prominent African-American film actors in the early days of Hollywood, but was only able to sustain an acting career once she gained weight and learned to speak with a backwoods dialect—elements that studio executives believed audiences wanted to see in their African-American characters.

2

Comfort Roles

African Americans survived the painful process of emancipation, but the portrayal of black culture by minstrels penetrated deeply into the American perspective. In the fifty years following the Emancipation Proclamation and the end of the Civil War, Jim Crow laws attempted to deal with the growing tide of African-American urbanization and the slowly growing sophistication of the black consumer. Once the first moving pictures—which were silent—reached the big screen, the image of the black in America was a disturbing mix of noble savage and comic servant.

"Anthropological" movies, detailing the "progress" of the races, were often outrageously bigoted. Claiming to represent genuine slices of life, they drew heavily on the stereotypes of the African American as exotic, comic, violent, and childlike, drawing heavily on the minstrel fabrications of an earlier era. Films like *The Birth of a Nation* were openly racist justifications of why blacks should be prevented from penetrating the social and financial arena.

Even movies with abolitionist themes, like *Uncle Tom's Cabin*, which was based on the book by Harriet Beecher Stowe, did not give the genuine African American much of a leg up. *Uncle Tom's Cabin* was first filmed in 1903, but it was not until 1914 that a black actor, Sam Lucas, starred in any version. White men made up in blackface—a holdover minstrel tradition—accounted for the black characters in earlier versions of the film. Thus, there were no blacks in leading roles in American film until 1914. And those who were later chosen for films still contended with the problem of their on-screen images. Americans wanted African Americans on screen, as they had been on stage, to meet certain comforting stereotypes.

Louise Beavers, one of the most important African-American actresses in the first half of the twentieth century, spent much of her career confronting the demands of a bigoted public. Her first big break, a role in *Uncle Tom's Cabin*, was reduced to that of a cook, because she did not have quite the bulk or age to be the stereotypically overweight maid. In order to work steadily, she forced herself to eat until she met the comfort level of the audience, who wanted a very dark-skinned, ample domestic on film.

Beavers was also not "folksy" enough. She was a transplant to Los Angeles from Cincinnati, and did not speak in the backwoods dialects of a Southern mammy. Consequently she trained herself to do so. She also taught herself to look happy cooking, although she detested food preparation, in order to ensure a steady stream of work cast as a jolly black cook, as Donald Bogle recorded.

She was then cast in a lengthy list of primarily servant roles. In 1931, she starred in *Annabelle's Affairs*, *Girls Around Town*, and *Sundown Trail*. She made ten more films in 1932, including two for famed director George Cukor—*What Price Hollywood* and *Divorce In the Family*. Bigger successes followed, as she played the servant Pearl in *She Done Him Wrong* with Mae West and the servant Loretta in *Bombshell* with Jean Harlow. She did seven more films in 1933, and then she was given a part in *Imitation of Life*. During filming, she and the National Association for the Advancement of Colored People successfully petitioned for the removal of an offensive racial slur from the script. Her bravery did not go unpunished. She was made to pronounce the word "Negro" repeatedly for studio executives, and her fine performance in *Imitation of Life* failed to win her an Academy Award nomination, despite it being called "the finest performance of 1934."

Perhaps because of the difficulty engendered by *Imitation of Life*, her next film, *Rainbow on the River*, contains a "shameless" scene where she argues that a slave in the Civil War never wanted freedom anyway. From this performance, she followed with a series of servant roles in films like *Make Way for Tomorrow*, *Wings Over Honolulu*, *Love in a Bungalow*, *The Last Gangster*, *Scandal Street*, *Life Goes On*, *Peck's Bad Boy with the Circus*, and *The Lady's From Kentucky*.

In 1939 she starred in David O. Selznick's *Made For Each Other*, a higher quality film in which she conveyed a moving level of Christian stoicism as she comforted Depression victims James Stewart and Carole Lombard. She worked steadily throughout the 1940s—primarily in servant roles—and appeared in *Shadow of the Thin Man*, *Reap the Wild Wind*, *DuBarry Was a Lady*, *Jack London*, and *Mr. Blandings Builds His Dream House* with Cary Grant. In the 1950s, she acted in *The Jackie Robinson Story*, and then took over the title role on *Beulah* as the maid on the fledgling medium of television. Her last film roles were *Teen-Age Rebel*, *Tammy and the Bachelor*, *The Goddess*, *All the Fine Young Cannibals*, and *The Facts of Life*. Throughout her career she played a black domestic, loving and supporting the more central figures of a white family.

She was one of many African Americans interested in film who found themselves limited by what studio executives believed fit the desires of American consumers. The flagrantly servile onscreen persona of Stepin Fetchit, for example, was popular throughout the entire nation in the 1930s. Fetchit, whose real name was Lincoln Theodore Monroe Andrew Perry, was featured in a number of outrageously stereotyped roles as an inept, shuffling servant. He was a foil for white comic icons such as Will Rogers, and can be seen in such degrading fare as *Charlie Chan in Egypt* and *On the Avenue.* Altogether he made twenty-six films, often working on as many as four at a time. Perry was the best known and most successful African-American actor working in Hollywood. He was, for example, the first Negro to receive featured billing.

Fetchit played essentially the same character in all of those films, as did his later imitators, Mantan Moreland and Willie Best (demeaningly called "Sleep 'n' Eat"). Fetchit was a bumbling servant in *In Old Kentucky* (1927), *The Ghost Talks* (1929), *Show Boat* (1929), and *Fox Movietone Follies* (1929). He was tricked into believing he was a talking penguin and that people thought him a French man in *The World Moves On* (1934) and *David Harum* (1934). In the films he made with Will Rogers, Stepin Fetchit sunk to subhuman levels, as Donald Bogle notes. In one, he was traded to Will Rogers along with a horse, and later traded back again. This slavery disguised as comedy ran through the entire film.

He continued this characterization in *Judge Priest* (1934), *The County Chairman* (1935), and *Steamboat 'Round the Bend* (1935). The master/servant interplay was the core of his remaining body of work, including *Helldorado, One More Spring, 36 Hours to Kill, Dimples, On The Avenue, Zenobia, Salute, Bend of the River,* and *The Sun Shines Bright.*

His presence in films like the Charlie Chan series—roles taken over first by Willie Best and then by Mantan Moreland—beg another question: why did African Americans take these roles, which clearly did the race "a lot more harm than good," as Roland Vaughan commented? Fetchit, for example, was considered the "representative of the American Negro" by white film audiences for his on-screen roles as a lazy, sneaky, forgetful, good-for-nothing lackey.

The answer lies, again, in the perception of the consumer. Studios believed that Americans wanted these stereotypes, and

Stepin Fetchit in *Hearts of Dixie*. Fetchit was one of the most popular and successful African-American actors in film during the 1930s, but the characters he portrayed were often less than noble and dignified.

therefore would pay to see them. According to Donald Bogle, "Hollywood had found a new place for the Negro—in the kitchens, laundry rooms, and pantries. And thus was born the age of the Negro servant."

African Americans who wanted to act had few choices. African Americans who wanted access to *la dolce vita* conformed to what was expected of them. Stepin Fetchit, for example, lived a wildly extravagant off-screen lifestyle that left him four million dollars in debt, which was unimaginable to the average African American at that time. Also to be considered is the fact that if all black actors and actresses had taken the moral high road and refused to be in these movies, there would have been virtually no body of African-American film from this era. Some truly fine performances, such as Hattie McDaniel's Academy Award-winning turn as Scarlet O'Hara's maid in *Gone With the Wind*, would have been lost.

Hattie McDaniel herself succinctly summed up the situation of African Americans in Hollywood in the first half of the twentieth century, asking, "Why should I complain about making seven thousand dollars a week playing a maid? If I didn't, I'd be making seven dollars a week actually being one!"

But in Hattie McDaniel's hands, even those stereotyped maids became rich creations. "Hi-Hat Hattie," as she was called, became an overweight servant figure whose broad comic and maternal power simply overwhelmed the screen. Her domestics evolved into central figures in any scene she was given, marvelous in her wit and audacity. In her early films, *The Gold West* (1932) and *Blonde Venus* (1932) and *The Story of Temple Drake* (1933), McDaniel follows the script and plays a loyal, hardly distinguishable servant. But, in *Judge Priest* (1934), despite the strong stereotyped performances by Stepin Fetchit and Will Rogers, McDaniels pioneered the character of the outspoken, aggressively no-nonsense black woman. "Come on here while I holler at you," she snaps at Fetchit. Aficionados of modern television sitcoms will have no trouble recognizing this servant-who-is-not-servile character, from the maid in *The Jeffersons* to the governor's assistant in *Benson*.

This fearlessness also streaks 1934's *Operator 13*, *Lost In the Stratosphere*, and *Little Men*, and 1935's *Music Is Magic*, *Another Face*, *China Seas* and *The Little Colonel*. But, in 1935, she broke out into full glory in George Stevens' *Alice Adams*, acting opposite Katherine Hepburn and Fred MacMurray. Her comic turn as a hired maid who doesn't think much of the white character's pretenses became a classic. No filmgoer doubted that McDaniel considered herself an equal, servant role or not.

Hattie McDaniel with Vivien Leigh in *Gone With The Wind*. Her portrayals of sassy servants were very popular, and she even won an Academy Award for Best Supporting Actress for her work in *Gone With The Wind* —making her the first African American to win an Oscar.

In 1936, McDaniel was so popular that she appeared in eleven movies. They were *Gentle Julia, The First Baby, Show Boat, Hearts Divided, High Tension, Postal Inspector, Star For The Night, Reunion, The Bride Walks Out, Valiant is the Word For Carrie,* and *Can This Be Dixie?* She made seven more films in 1937, establishing great rapport with Clark Gable in *Saratoga.* By the late 1930s, the movies she made with such luminaries as Barbara Stanwyck provided roles tailor-made for her confident, no-nonsense trademark persona. She had become the nurturing servant for an entire nation. And for that, she was the first African American given an Academy Award for Best Supporting Actress in 1939's David O. Selznick's Civil War epic *Gone With The Wind.*

Another African-American actress, Butterfly McQueen, also distinguished herself in *Gone With the Wind*, playing the delicate, fearful Prissy. Just as McDaniel's servant role allowed anger to surface, powerfully representing repressed understanding of the wrongs suffered at the hands of white America, Prissy gave fear an outlet. In the hands of lesser actresses, the shades of feeling may have been lost and the roles may have been reduced to mere stereotypes, but Hattie McDaniels and Butterfly McQueen evoke deeper and more complex emotions.

They did not stand alone. Paul Robeson, the son of a former slave, was a formidable intellectual who had won a scholarship to Rutgers University in 1915, becoming only the third African American at the time to ever do so. He overcame overt racism in order to graduate Phi Beta Kappa and as the valedictorian of his class. He received a law degree from Columbia University in 1923, but quit his law firm in New York when a white secretary would not allow him to dictate to her. He married Eslanda Cardozo Goode, the first black woman ever to head a pathology laboratory. In 1924, he performed in Eugene O'Neill's *All God's Chillun Got Wings*, a daring work regarding racism that created much controversy. He went on to star in another O'Neill vehicle, *Emperor Jones*, attracting more attention.

Robeson was a black artist whose innate dignity and personal achievement made him first a star and then a target for an America unready to champion civil liberty. At first, Robeson— who was a former All-American football player—intrigued America. He was proud, and not servile. He worked in foreign pictures which he felt afforded less stereotyping. He walked out in protest when roles were rewritten behind his back. In *The Emperor Jones*, one of his best-known roles, he is assertive and defiant.

American audiences, however, rejected Robeson after a sadly short span of work because of his association with Communism. Uneasy with his concept of equality and all that it implied, Robeson was essentially blacklisted for his political views, a foretaste of the anti-Communist hysteria that would reach its peak in the 1950s. His last film was such a dismal affront to civil rights groups that after Robeson himself had seen a complete version, he joined the protesters in speaking out against it.

Mainstream white America, however, was not ready for an independently minded African-American artist. It would be many years before the sterotypes fostered by the minstrel shows began to crumble significantly. Artists like Robeson were a threat to the belief in white superiority, and like many other talented Negro performers, he was virtually exiled to a more liberal political climate during the prime of his life.

Oscar Micheaux was an independent filmmaker who attempted to make films—later known as "race movies"—that gave a different portrayal of African Americans than that of the Hollywood studios. These movies would be shown late at night—the only time African Americans were allowed to attend movie theaters.

3

An Actor's Anxiety

African Americans were ready for a more realistic portrayal of their experiences, even if the majority of white America was being spoonfed updated minstrel images. As a result, black-market midnight theater, featuring movies made primarily by African Americans for African Americans, developed into a distinct subculture in the hands of talented independent film-makers like Oscar Micheaux, Noble Johnson, William Foster, and Emmett J. Scott. Sometimes called race movies, these attempts to portray blacks as something other than buffoons or savages flourished outside of the mainstream cinema during the 1920s and 1930s.

Foster was the first to raise enough money to make small-budget, all-black films beginning with *The Railroad Porter* in 1912. He also produced *The Fall Guy* and *The Barber*, as well as various features starring the characters "Buck" and "Bubbles." Then, in 1914, Biograph

Pictures of New York made *A Natural Born Gambler,* starring Bert Williams. Heartened by these small successes, entrepreneurs began in earnest to try to attract black audiences to black stars.

Some of these entrepreneurs had a higher purpose than pure commercialism. Booker T. Washington's secretary, Emmett J. Scott, made an epic black film, *The Birth of A Race* (formerly titled *Lincoln's Dream*), as a reaction to the blatantly racist film *The Birth of a Nation,* a production with Ku Klux Klan backing that was protested vigorously by the National Association for the Advancement of Colored People (NAACP). The three-hour film opened at Blackstone Theater in Chicago in 1918.

It was not a commercial success. However, it paved the way for the Lincoln Motion Picture Company, founded by black actor Noble P. Johnson and his brother, George. The Johnsons adeptly kept their films short, their material attention-getting, and their productions numerous. Their success inspired others, and more black filmmakers, like the legendary Oscar Micheaux, began to create features for the seven hundred or so black theaters that eventually sprang up around the country in the first half of the twentieth century.

The so-called midnight movies did not always dispel racism or avoid stereotypes entirely, but they were a landmark attempt to give human dignity and a broader range to the all-black characters onscreen. These films, which were shown late at night since that was the only time African Americans were allowed to frequent most theaters, were successful enough to employ a large number of black actors and actresses, including Mantan Moreland, Louise Beavers, Nina Mae McKinney, Eddie Anderson, Spencer Williams, and Lena Horne.

The performances of black entertainers in these films

curiously underscore the professionalism of African Americans, including those who acted in demeaning roles in mainstream American film. For example, Mantan Moreland, who portrayed the most bumbling sidekick in the Charlie Chan series, was known to white audiences far and wide for his ridiculous, cowardly, demented characters. His short stature made him seem even more like a mascot for his white handler, to whom he was always faithful although he was inevitably in the wrong place at the wrong time. Moreland gave so many of these minstrel-like performances that his image was synonymous with the comic servant. Once he had been "discovered" more or less in 1938 for his performances in films such as *Irish Luck, Frontier Scout,* and *Next Time I Marry,* he worked steadily in such Charlie Chan movies as *The Chinese Cat* (1944), *The Scarlet Clue* (1945), *The Jade Mask* (1945), *Shadow Over Chinatown* (1946), and *The Chinese Ring* (1947). He also played more or less the same absurd character in *Sarong Girl* (1943), *Revenge of the Zombies* (1943), *Melody Parade* (1943), and *South of Dixie* (1944). But Moreland, like the other African-American actors of his generation, was capable of a great deal more.

All-black movies shown at midnight to all-black audiences showcased a different side of Moreland. In 1939, an independent black filmmaker produced *One Dark Night,* featuring Moreland as a father out of work. His sensitive, pathetic, and finally heroic performance demonstrated that his range was far more extensive than the demeaning sidekick roles to which he was relegated in mainstream white film. Moreland himself thought *One Dark Night* was his best performance. He also starred in an all-black version of Samuel Beckett's absurdist drama *Waiting For Godot* (1957).

All-black films arose from an unmet need in mainstream cinema, but mainstream cinema itself was being shaped by the changing sophistication of its audience. For example, in 1915, when the first black film companies were employing black casts, a movie called *Free and Equal* was produced but not released until 1925. In *Free and Equal,* a black man is introduced into a Northern white liberal's home, where he proceeds to woo the white daughter, and rape and strangle the maid. Then, proof of his marriage to a black woman is produced. The simmering anti-black hostility and the ridiculous blackface alienated the audiences of 1925, who now preferred their racism sugarcoated with comedy.

For half a century thereafter, whenever the life of the African American was depicted on film in anything other than this comic vein, it was generally to indulge the mainstream audience with sentimental tragedy. The last gasp of the blackface minstrel tradition, Al Jolson's *The Jazz Singer,* exploited this vein of pathos shamelessly and successfully, but the advent of sound mercifully killed the blackface convention. And ironically, racism also helped. Talking pictures opened up the possibility of big production musicals, and Depression-era audiences warmed up quickly to the lavish escapist spectacles mounted by Hollywood picture companies like Fox and MGM. African Americans, reputed to be full of natural rhythm, attracted the attention of movie moguls looking to score with dazzling productions.

Hearts in Dixie and *Hallelujah* were instant successes. *Hearts in Dixie* (1929) directly borrowed all of the old minstrel show standbys, with happy blacks working in cotton fields in a nostalgic deference to slavery. The blacks sang joyfully throughout the movie, with no apparent suffering at the hands of overseers, slavecatchers, yellow fever, or any of the other countless tragedies that faced the actual plantation worker of the antebellum South. Nevertheless, mainstream critics rhapsodized over the portrayals, calling *Hearts in Dixie* ". . . restful, a talking and singing picture that is gentle in mood and truthful in its recollection of black men of those days down yonder in the cornfields." The happy-go-lucky servants apparently did not require any pity.

Hallelujah, in contrast, indulged the audience in high tragedy, with a troubled colored boy going wrong and a "yaller gal" (a light-skinned African American) charming the men. The role of the mulatto in Hollywood, as in the rest of the United States, was uneasy. Women of mixed ancestry, like Nina Mae McKinney and Lena Horne, were apt to be considered intrinsically more spiritual than a darker skinned African American, but nevertheless too tainted with animalism to overcome the appetites that lead to her downfall. At best, she is aware that she is a tragic figure as she flaunts herself through a film. *Hallelujah* was nevertheless banned by the Southern Theatre Federation for starring a black lead.

Nina Mae McKinney, at seventeen years old, played the first black prostitute in films. Her role in *Hallelujah* lifted her from the chorus in Lew Leslie's *Blackbirds* revue. Director King Vidor himself spotted her, and she was considered one of the great discoveries of the time period. MGM signed her to a five-year contract. Then, disappointingly, she discovered that there were no leading lady roles in Hollywood for a black woman, even one that looked marginally white. Nina Mae McKinney became a nightclub singer in Europe, just as Josephine Baker had, performing in cabarets and nightclubs in Paris, London, Budapest, Greece, and Dublin. Her moniker, the "Black Garbo," extended the mysterious, tragic mulatto persona built by the mainstream studios.

While in Europe, she starred in *Sanders of the River* with the equally disenfranchised leading man Paul Robeson. She returned to the United States to work in all-black productions and did not significantly reappear in mainstream film until 1949's *Pinky*, where she once again played the role of a mulatto. Disillusioned, she died in 1967, only 55 years old.

A scene from the 1929 movie *Hallelujah*, which was one of the first to feature the persona of the tragic mulatto, played here by Nina Mae McKinney. The movie was banned by the Southern Theatre Federation for having an African American in the lead.

The swaggering, hip-rolling, exotic vamp character she first embodied in *Hallelujah* lives on, though. In *Carmen Jones*, African-American actress Dorothy Dandridge unconsciously mimics McKinney, as did Mae West, Jean Harlow, and a host of other important American actresses. Unlike the mulatto actresses, the white performers did not have to end each role with tragedy, because their sexuality was not ultimately as threatening to the public perception. Even a beautiful young woman was dangerous if she was African American. The stereotypes of mainstream American show business provided a comfort zone for viewers used to living with prejudice.

Amos (Freeman Gosden) and Andy (Charles Corell) were two characters on a radio program of the same name who were played by white actors. Eventually the overwhelming success of the program gave way to television as well, though African-American attorneys and the NAACP tried to stop the show from continuing.

4

Old School Concept

Radio was little different from film when it came to perpetuating minstrel show stereotypes. The great age of radio programming, beginning in the 1940s, relied heavily on the image of the "sambo," or dupe, and the "dandy," or con man, whenever an African American was represented. The derogatory names came from early characters brought to stage by "Daddy" Rice, the blackface white performer who gave America Jim Crow. Rice also created "Jim Dandy" and "Zip Coon." The most flagrant example of the continuity of these minstrel show caricatures—and the most beloved—was *Amos 'n' Andy*, one of the highest-rated radio shows of all time. The controversial broadcast influenced American show business for nearly fifty years.

Just as they did in film, African Americans had a difficult time finding any roles, let alone roles of substance, in radio. Black radio actors faced an even greater hurdle than those in film. Because performers on radio were only heard and not seen, most of the African-American roles were played by whites. No blackface—which was rejected fairly decisively by the movie viewers of the 1920s—was even needed to help radio stations preserve the color barrier. And in the hands of a non-black performer, there was no limit to the indignity a black radio character could suffer in the name of "comedy."

Mainstream America loved it. On March 19, 1928, "Famous Amos" and "Handy Andy" were born on the airwaves as the creations of WMAQ's Freeman Gosden and Charles Correll. Gosden and Correll, both white, were hailed as "public gods." Sixty percent of America tuned in regularly to listen to a simple-minded, trusting Amos play off of the bossy, shiftless Andy. By 1931 more than 31 million people listened daily. Historians credit this astonishing demographic to the Depression, a time of such economic bleakness that Americans both identified with—and escaped with—the exploits of two black Southerners looking for work in the North.

The situation represented comforting familiarity as well as perpetuating stereotypes drawn from the minstrel era. After World War II, large numbers of African Americans did in fact migrate from the South to the North in search of work. The forerunner of *Amos 'n' Andy*, also created by Gosden and Correll, was based on this very scenario. The characters were named "Sam" and "Henry," and their adventures were told in serial form.

Sam 'n' Henry was originally conceived as a "black-voice" radio show in the early 1920s when blackface shows still enjoyed some popularity, or at least still traveled the country. The radio show was a solid link between this minstrel tradition and the later success of "odd couple" comedy pairings, like *Amos 'n' Andy* or the 1998 film *Rush Hour* with Chris Tucker and Jackie Chan. *Sam 'n' Henry* premiered on January 12, 1926, and it was unusual because it made use of the serial form to hook listeners night after night.

Whatever else Gosden and Carroll's creations were, they soon became symbolic figures. Even ministers in pulpits used the characters to illustrate their lessons, ameliorating the offensiveness of Amos' gullibility by stressing his honesty and loyalty. Amos, though black and at the mercy of elements well beyond his meager powers, was the Everyman. Jack Slater of *Emmy Magazine* observed that the show "became identified with the Great Depression." Americans could suffer along with the everhopeful black characters, and then push them away when they got too close to the bone. The comedy insulated a country from the shock of national events.

The show was so popular that phrases from it, such as "check and double check" and "I'se regusted," became part of the American idiom. The *St. Paul News* even wrote, "The stock market may crash and millionaires be made paupers, but these events pale away into trivial insignificance before the nationwide upheaval caused by the changes in time of the 'Amos 'n' Andy' broadcast." There are no figures available to show if the audience was composed only of whites—this seems unlikely.

Nevertheless, the cringe-worthy nature of much of the comedy could not be eased by the simple mythical attempt to provide lessons in right and wrong. Protests of the show began as little as two weeks after its premiere. Black attorneys filed injunctions to stop the performance of the show to no avail. Gosden and Correll hotly denied that their characters were anything but lovable. Gosden even claimed, "We have a deep respect for the black man. We feel our show helps characterize Negroes as interesting and dignified human beings."

At first, there weren't even any actual African Americans associated with the program cast. Gosden himself played Amos, using a high-pitched voice that he and many listeners found hysterically funny. Correll was Andy, and he would put his mouth very close to the mic to imitate what he thought of as black dialect. Andy repeatedly had to "'splain" concepts to Amos, who in many ways might have been a stand-in for an audience less sophisticated than the radio hosts themselves. America itself learned how to buy a car "on time," as well as other concepts, from Andy.

The real problem lay in the victimizing and exaggerated stupidity that the radio stations did not seem comfortable crediting in such a degree to white characters. As Bart Andrews and Ahrgus Juilliard state in the book *Holy Mackerel! The Amos 'n' Andy Story*, "As lovable and funny as Amos and Andy were, they were considered objectionable because they represented the *only* depiction of black life on the radio." The NAACP stated baldly, "The sooner they're off the air, the better it will be for the Negro. Radio points to one side of the Negro, the worst side, most frequently."

In fact, some changes were slowly occurring on the airwaves, although it took many years for their impact to even slightly alter African-American images on-screen. An African-American actor named Eddie Anderson played a controversial role in jumpstarting the process. Most famous for his role as Jack Benny's sidekick Rochester, Anderson's comic portrayal is credited with reviving Benny's flagging career and vaulting Benny to the heights in the fledgling years of television.

Eddie Anderson was a struggling actor with several film roles of little note when he was "discovered" by Jack Benny in 1937. The tales of his discovery differ—one places him as a newspaper carrier, one as a train porter—but both are likely untrue. Anderson had, after all, appeared in quite a few films, if only to say "Yessim." He had roles in *What Price Hollywood, Rainbow on the River, Three Men on a Horse, Melody for Two, Bill Cracks Down, On Such A Night, White Bondage, One Mile From Heaven*, and *Jezebel*. He had slightly more developed roles in *The Green Pastures* and W.C. Fields' *You Can't Cheat An Honest Man*, but his fortunes—as well as

Eddie Anderson rehearsing with Jack Benny in 1947. Anderson was credited to reviving Benny's career, and gave a twist to the servant role of Rochester, who was actually not servile or thickheaded at all—instead, he was the wisest of all the characters.

Benny's—improved dramatically after they paired up in film and in radio.

The teaming began on radio with Rochester playing Benny's shrewd—and *not* subservient—gentleman's gentleman. The audience was shown that Rochester's servant character was really in charge of the house, and that his advice to Benny invariably turned out to be correct despite some tomfoolery. An important change took place here, as Donald Bogle notes. Rochester "rose above the old tradition because at heart his humor—along with the warmth and affection he engendered in his audience—was based more on his wisecracks and his shrewdness than on his color."

The response to this venture was encouraging enough that Rochester actually developed an on-screen love life with actress Theresa Harris. He also was given the lead in *Cabin In the Sky*, the black musical produced for mainstream film. He played, with amazing ability, Little Joe Jackson, foolishly lured away from his good wife Petunia by the lovely Lena Horne, a mixed race actress who was the most popular African-American leading lady during the war years.

Lena Horne, in fact, was a songstress rather than an actress. She appeared at the famous Cotton Club in Harlem at the young age of sixteen, and followed that up with the revue by Lew Leslie called *Blackbirds*. When big budget Hollywood turned to big musical numbers inserted in films, her career really exploded. Posed dramatically, she would enter a film as a nightclub singer in segments which could easily be edited out for the film's debut in the South.

Lena Horne's film career spanned the range of the 1940s with such pictures as *Panama Hattie* (1942), *I Dood It*, *Swing Fever* (1943), *Broadway Rhythm of 1944*, *Two Girls and A Sailor* (1944), *Ziegfeld Follies* (1944), *Till the Clouds Roll By* (1946), *Words and Music* (1948) and *Duchess of Idaho* (1950).

However, her great success in film may have been cut short by her activism. Horne was active in the Council for African Affairs and friendly with Paul Robeson, and was subsequently blacklisted—her name appeared in the Red Channels, a published report listing entertainers and organizations considered to be "subversive." The anti-Communist hysteria of the 1950s, coupled with the fear of an empowered African American, lost her roles until the late fifties and early sixties.

The roles for African Americans in film and radio were thus clearly defined by prejudice. In fact, black radio performers were required to speak in the way white people believed a Southern rural black talked. This stereotype was so strong, in fact, that according to Andrews and Juilliard, "If a black performer could not master the minstrel accent, he lost his job." Apparently, this is what happened to Red Skelton show cast member "Wonderful" Smith, a black actor who didn't sound "black enough." And despite the fact that performers on radio couldn't be seen, they were only able to play black characters, although white actors regularly masqueraded as blacks on the airwaves. Prejudice was a dominant factor shaping the entertainment business.

The one break African Americans had on radio—which was ironically rooted in racial stereotyping—was that radio shows featuring black musicians flourished, as blacks were reputed to possess a natural rhythm more strongly than whites. Black performers like the Mills Brothers, the Ink Spots, Bob Howard, and Adelaide Hall hosted programs enjoyed by an entire nation. Duke Ellington created a show for NBC, and Louis Armstrong had a network series sponsored by Fleischmann's Yeast, much as *Amos 'n' Andy* had featured advertisements for Pepsodent. Gospel music was also a popular radio feature. As early as the 1920s, black singers had performed for radio, including the Pace Jubilee Negro Singers, Fess Williams, and Noble Sissle.

General Electric, Kodak, and other advertisers sponsored shows which showcased Ethel Waters, Fats Waller, Nina Mae McKinney, Art Tatum, the Four Southern Singers, the Four Sheiks of Harmony, the Babolene Boys, Jules Bledsoe, as well as musicians like Chick Webb, Don Redman, and Cab Calloway. African-American radio performers drew millions of American

The Ink Spots were one of the many African-American musical acts to be featured on major radio programs, and they were immensely popular. Strangely enough, the racial stereotype that blacks inherently had more rhythm than whites helped boost their popularity, and the interest and controversy surrounding "race music" (as it was called then) continues to this very day.

listeners, beginning a nationwide interest in—and controversy regarding—so-called "race music." This controversy eventually culminated in the birth of rock and roll in the 1950s, one of the formative events in American popular culture. The history of African Americans in the entertainment industry has always provided an important barometer of American attitudes of the time.

Oscar winner Hattie McDaniel went on to play the title role in the TV series *Beulah*. Originally a radio program, *Beulah* told the story of a wise black housekeeper working for a white family. Interestingly, McDaniel left the show, and was eventually replaced by Louise Beavers—who was told yet again to gain more weight for a role!

5

Small Screen Politics

Radio material, which drew its characterizations from minstrel shows just as early film had done, developed into basic television in the early 1950s. Some shows, like *Amos 'n' Andy*, moved directly to the small screen, necessitating a changeover to black actors but not much of a change in outlook. Other characters, most notably the African-American servant, transferred also.

Non-fictitious black characters also appeared with greater frequency on television. They became fixtures on music programming, sports, and occasionally on quiz shows. Thanks to radio, African-American sports figures like boxer Joe Louis already inspired a nation with their prowess, and the entire American filmgoing audience had waited breathlessly for the victory of Jesse Owens at the Berlin Olympics, competing in the face of Hitler's overt racism. Americans may have been prejudiced, but they certainly did not like to think of themselves that way. Black television characters, therefore, were viewed with genuine affection, even if they were not human beings who were able to realize a full range of human potential. The beloved black nurturing, full-figured female of books and movies translated itself into several ongoing television characters.

One of the most popular was *Beulah*. Beulah was the housekeeper for a white family, the Hendersons, and she never failed to solve their problems by the end of an episode. *Beulah* began on radio as part of the NBC radio program called *Homeward Unincorporated* (1939). The character of the buxom, cheerful, loving maid proved so successful that it appeared on other radio programs, including 1943's *That's Life* and *Fibber McGee and Molly*. In 1945, the character of Beulah got its own radio program on CBS.

The first Beulah was actually played by white male actor Marlin Hurt, whose thick fake Southern accent was ridiculous. Hurt died in 1940, and his role was taken by Bob Corley. It was not until 1947 that an African-American woman, Hattie McDaniel, took over the characterization. McDaniel of course had won a Best Supporting Actress Oscar for *Gone With The Wind* in 1939 for playing a servant role.

The change to an African-American actress in the part was spurred by the end of World War II. Fought by all Americans, black and white, returning African-American soldiers questioned their place in post-war society. In 1948, President Harry Truman, reflecting the greater tolerance of American society in the wake of the Second World War, became the first president to encourage legislation to end racial discrimination. Poets like Langston Hughes, writing movingly of "A Dream Deferred," were beginning to raise the consciousness of educated Americans, and a limited reassessment of the African-American place in America gained momentum. The writer Gwendolyn Brooks won a Pulitzer prize; Ralphe Bunche won the Nobel Peace prize. It was harder to convince the American public that the African American was the buffoon of early film and radio.

The results were felt in the entertainment industry. Black

characters were included, even embraced, and their images evolved from the simpletons and villains of earlier days, but the evolution stopped far short of equality. Black women like Beulah were still servants, but now they were shrewd servants, much like Eddie Anderson's Rochester. The maid and the valet saved the white family's bacon week after week, apparently without much ambition for themselves. Outside of the family but familiar, they reflected the deceptive "separate but equal" doctrine that was finding favor in the rest of American society. Americans used television to hide their racism from themselves. Americans did not want to think of themselves like Hitler.

Meanwhile, the *Beulah* show transferred from the radio to television with a cast change—the New York-based Ethel Waters was cast by ABC as the leading figure, replacing McDaniel. Butterfly McQueen, who had also acted in *Gone With The Wind* with McDaniel, played Beulah's friend Oriole, who still retained the high-pitched voice and antic comedy which drew its power from the minstrel show. Percy "Bud" Harris, eventually replaced by Dooley Wilson, played Beulah's boyfriend, Bill. The white Henderson family, consisting of parents with a little boy named Donnie, were initially played by William Post Jr., Ginger Jones, and Clifford Sales.

The cast underwent more changes, but the characterizations remained predictable. Louise Beavers took over the role of Beulah, and the Hendersons too were replaced by Jane Frazee, David Bruce, and Stuffy Singer. Darker skin and ample weight were considered less threatening to the viewing public, and Beavers was encouraged to add more heft to her frame. Clearly, television stations like radio stations were sensitive to the concerns of their mainstream viewers, as well as their sponsors. Stations in the South faced particularly thorny problems. Matters came to a terrible head on *The Nat "King" Cole Show.*

In 1956, Nat "King" Cole's fifteen-minute variety program debuted. It was the only network series at the time to star an

African American. Bob Howard, Hazel Scott, and Billy Daniels, for example, had hosted shows before, but Cole was given the assurance of a weekly program. Cole was a singer whose style more resembled Frank Sinatra and Bing Crosby than the growing group of rock and roll singers who were frightening the more conservative members of the American public. It was considered a progressive but safe move to feature Cole performing pop tunes with guest stars like Pearl Bailey, Cab Calloway, Mahalia Jackson, Sammy Davis Jr., Mel Torme, Tony Bennett, Harry Belafonte and Peggy Lee.

Unfortunately, the ratings were not as high as NBC had hoped. Faced with stiff competition from CBS's *The Adventures of Robin Hood, The Nat "King" Cole* show only drew in about 19 percent of the television audience. Big name stars like Sammy Davis Jr. and Mahalia Jackson, in an effort to help the ailing show, performed for far less than their standard wages—accepting, respectively, a Leica camera and a color television set in payment.

The question of why the show was placed in the time slot that it was given and was offered for much cheaper rates to advertisers was a source of some bitterness for Cole. He felt that the advertising gurus of Madison Avenue were not willing to shape a more equal world by putting their money behind black performers. The entertainment establishment itself responded with the justification that they were concerned their sponsors would not accept a show with an African-American lead, particularly in the South. Sadly, the prediction proved true. In Birmingham, Alabama, a station manager was pressured to drop the show under the threat that if he didn't, his house and station would be bombed. The controversy raged on until *The Nat "King" Cole* show was finally moved to a more amenable time slot. It rose to the number one position in New York and number eight in Los Angeles—a strong showing. Clearly the niche for the variety show starring an African American was urban and not rural.

In an effort to bridge the ever-widening gap between civil rights

The movie *The Green Pastures* appeared on television in 1957 and was a great success. Unfortunately, the show recalled sentimental portrayals of African Americans from earlier Broadway musicals and minstrel shows. In this all-black version of Heaven, God was known as "De Lawd."

activism and the conservative old Southern mentality during the same year that *The Nat "King" Cole* show was cancelled, NBC produced an all-black *Hallmark Hall of Fame* movie entitled *The Green Pastures* (1957). The show looked back wistfully to Depression-era Broadway and minstrel images from the nineteenth-century South. *The Green Pastures* imagined an all-black Heaven, with cute little black cherubs and an abundance of fish fries and custard pudding. Omnipotence was represented by "De Lawd," played by William Warfield. Eddie Anderson was Noah, Frederick O'Neal played Moses, Richard Ward was Pharoah, and Terry Carter acted the role of Gabriel. Earle Hyman, who many years later would play the father of Bill Cosby's groundbreaking Dr. Huxtable character on *The Cosby Show*, played both Adam and Hezdrel.

The production, which was an instant success with critics, was again unthreatening and pastoral, purportedly in folksy black style. *New York Times* critic Jack Gould felt that *The Green Pastures* "contained some of the season's finest acting." In fact, the production was enough of a success with mainstream America that a second, live version of *The Green Pastures* was rebroadcast almost two years later. Blacks were allowed to be on the American conscience; they just weren't allowed to be fully human.

When America explored the "Negro Dilemma" in the late 1940s and 1950s, it was with a series of stock and troubling images. The anger which America was beginning to realize lay just beneath the surface of the African-American experience was represented on screen by character types that menaced the fabric of a wholesome society. Black women who would not be servants were Jezebels, dangerous fantasy playthings whose darker skin clearly made their beauty threatening, and their fate inevitably tragic.

Dorothy Dandridge is a case in point. Born in Cleveland, Ohio, in 1922, Dandridge was the daughter of a domestic. Supposedly her first real film break came when she seduced Otto Preminger and won a lead role in the all-black production of *Carmen Jones*. Cast on-screen (as well as off) as a siren, Dandridge simmered on film and stage while enduring the humiliation of not being allowed in the white dressing room when she traveled with a production. Often she made do with a broom closet. Dandridge was the first black performer to play New York's prestigious Waldorf Astoria Hotel, but the white doormen probably had more freedom to enter the hotel.

Such ironies were not lost on the complicated and intelligent Dandridge. Like Josephine Baker and Nina Mae McKinney, from whom Dandridge derived some of her on-screen persona as a tragic and seductive mulatto, she had trouble sustaining a career as a leading lady in a country short of roles for African-American actresses. Her life was cut short when she overdosed on a prescription antidepressant. It is unknown if her death was an accident or a suicide.

Significantly, white women cast as mulattos had a better chance for happiness on screen. Natalie Wood, Ava Gardner, and Yvonne DeCarlo all played beautiful women with black blood, although none of the actresses was even partially African American. Hollywood producers felt that these women would appeal more to the mainstream audience while reaping sentimental tears over the race question. This position made it all the more difficult for African-American actresses to land meaty parts.

Because of the shortage of quality roles on screen for African-American performers, the nightclub circuit was a popular venue for sophisticated performers like Pearl Bailey, Sammy Davis Jr., and Hazel Scott. Hazel Scott was an original—difficult for filmmakers to exploit, unwilling to fit in a stereotype. A pianist born in Port of Spain, Trinidad, Scott exuded composed and cultured presence while displaying phenomenal skill at her instrument. Her style, a blend of classical with swing music, called attention to her versatility. Her demeanor was ladylike, yet unyielding: she refused to appear in films except as herself, seated at a piano, in order to avoid demeaning stereotypes. As a result, she was cast in fewer and fewer movies. Scott told *Ebony* magazine in 1944 that she did not choose to play either a sexual being or a servant, and there were few other roles available for black women outside of nightclub performance. She married the influential black politician Adam Clayton Powell in 1945, and her performing career came to a close. In 1981, Hazel Scott died, and was one of the few performers who had rarely made compromises to remain in the public spotlight.

Eartha Kitt had a catlike and fiery persona that didn't sit as well with the American mainstream as it had with nightclub and stage audiences. But she gave a very lively performance as Catwoman on the campy *Batman* television series in the 1960s.

Eartha Kitt also failed to fill a comforting niche on main-stream American screens in the 1950s, as Donald Bogle notes. He goes so far as to say that Kitt "lacked the conventional good looks that could make an audience take an interest in her no matter what she did. Easily intimidated audiences may have found her demonic and dangerous." Her catlike persona, slinky and independent, worked to her benefit on the nightclub circuit and on stage, where smaller and more sophisticated audiences appreciated her approach to performance. Her film career was short and unremarkable, with such pictures as *St. Louis Blues,* a fictional account of the life of black jazzman W.C. Handy; *New Faces of 1952*; *The Mark of the Hawk*; and *Anna Lucasta.* She did not become a national icon until her antic performance as Catwoman in the cartoonish 1960s television series *Batman*, starring Adam West.

Television in 1950s America was, at best, sanitized. At worst, it was a mirror for the segregation and stereotyping that had plagued black artists since the beginning of a distinctive American culture. The 1960s, though, saw the beginning of great social upheaval in America, and the new medium of television would be greatly affected.

Bill Cosby appeared with Robert Culp in the television series *I Spy*. African Americans were now taking lead roles in television series that were no longer demeaning or holdovers from the minstrel traditions. Instead, these characters were dignified and independent—no longer servants or bumbling fools.

6

A Revolution Is Televised

In the 1960s, America discovered a new use for the exciting medium of television: witnessing the nation's upheavals. The Civil Rights movement—with haunting images of fire hoses, police dogs, and dignified, brave African-American schoolgirls under fire from screaming white adults—played out on television. The conscience of a nation was stirred by the unquestionably factual images paraded on the news. Fiction on television had to be adjusted accordingly, although change when it came was slow and incomplete.

The revolution began with the appearance of African-American actors and actresses in lead roles on mainstream television: Bill Cosby in *I Spy* and Diahann Carroll in *Julia*. Black characters also were featured as regulars in ensemble casts, and their characterizations abandoned the old minstrel stereotypes. For example, Ivan Dixon appeared in *Hogan's Heroes*, Nichelle Nichols played Uhura on *Star Trek*, Hari Rhodes was featured in *Daktari*, Greg Morris starred in *Mission: Impossible*, and Clarence Williams III played Linc on *Mod Squad*. Each of these characters was presented as shrewd and self-confident. Their portrayals contained a serious undertone of dignity and even some threads of activism—these characters were nobody's servants.

However, Bill Cosby, who won an Emmy for Outstanding Actor in a Drama Series during the 1965-66 television season, was initially considered a bad choice for the role of agent Alexander Scott. Sheldon Leonard recalled to Donald Bogle that Cosby "was just what we needed for *I Spy*, except for one thing. He was black."

The networks, worried about losing sponsors, particularly in the South, pressured Leonard to replace Cosby, citing his inexperience as an actor. *I Spy* was Cosby's first acting job. Previously, he had crafted his characterizations onstage as a comedian. Leonard rightly felt that Cosby, given a fair chance, could demonstrate universal appeal. His decision eventually proved to be enormous.

Meanwhile, the show's developers were dealing with such race-laden issues during the day-to-day filming of *I Spy* as deciding how to placate Southern sponsors. Would they be offended to see the black and the white secret agent sitting in the front seat of a car together? Would the black agent be refused service in a hotel, as was likely in real life?

The last question, as were many others of this nature, was resolved by sidestepping the issue until the producers were comfortable with national response to the mixed-race team. The series, which featured international secret agents, was therefore set all over the world, in foreign hotels where viewers might not question if Bill Cosby's character stayed in the same hotel with Robert Culp's Agent Kelly Robinson. This technique served to keep the African American on television in a separate but equal position that fell short of genuine color-blindness. As Donald Bogle succinctly notes, "*I Spy* mostly kept the new Negro in foreign lands. So did *Mission: Impossible*. *Daktari* took the new Negro back to the dark continent. And *Star Trek* projected the new Negro into outer space." Integration had reached everywhere but twentieth-century America, apparently.

Then, producer and creator Hal Kanter sold a series to NBC television called *Julia*. *Julia* was played by Diahann Carroll, born Carol Diann Johnson on July 17, 1935. Carroll was first and foremost a singer, stating in her autobiography, "All I ever wanted to do was sing. What happened was more." She entered show business in her teens, a girl beautiful enough to model. She sang successfully in nightclubs and appeared on Broadway, although parts for black actresses and singers were few and far between. The situation on Broadway mirrored the rest of the entertainment industry. She described that industry in her own book: "In the beginning, I found myself dealing with a show business dictated by male white supremacists and chauvinists. As a black female, I had to learn how to tap dance around the situation. I had to . . . find a way to present my point of view without being pushy or aggressive."

This dismal situation existed for all women as well, not just black ones. For example, Carroll noted "in the old days, the only women I saw in this business were in makeup, hairdressing, and wardrobe departments." Carroll helped to change some of that inequity. Her show, *Julia,* was a good step towards the integration of television.

Julia was the story of a black nurse widowed by the Vietnam War, raising her young son in an integrated apartment building in Los Angeles. The concept was radical, and yet it drew fire from activists for not being edgy and real enough. The show was designed not to alienate mainstream viewers while still acknowledging the existence of prejudice—a tricky line to walk. Diahann Carroll found herself defending her series from day one on September 17, 1968. She perceptively pointed out that television is a business and part of the entertainment industry, and that all television series, featuring either black or white actors and actresses, were "divorced from reality" in more ways than they were attached.

Diahann Carroll starred in the television series *Julia*, which told the story of a nurse whose husband was killed in the Vietnam War, and who was raising her son in an integrated apartment building in Los Angeles. Her race, however, burdened the show with unrealistic expectations.

The *New York Daily News* echoed her cries, asking why Diahann Carroll's situation comedy should have to carry so much philosophical weight. If the show was about a white nurse, no one would expect anything more than fluffy comedy. But, with an African-American lead, said the reviewer, "the next thing we know Diahann will be asked not only to solve the racial question but even the Vietnam War . . . "

But all African Americans were burdened with the knowledge that in order for stereotypes to dissolve and genuine integration occur, visible black actors and actresses were unfairly stuck with the duty to represent an entire ethnic group in a highly public fashion. The National Association for the Advancement of Colored People (the NAACP) had grown into a powerful movement that was inspiring and pursuing equality across America. Lunchrooms were being forcibly integrated, as were schools, hotels, restaurants, and other public venues. Television, the most public venue of all, needed to follow suit in order to keep the momentum going. Therefore, blacks on-screen carried more than their share of the national conscience.

Some, like movie actor Sidney Poitier, took that role seriously and fulfilled it beyond expectation. His major roles included such dignified and poignant humanitarian standouts as *Cry, The Beloved Country*; *Lilies of the Field*; and *To Sir, With Love*. His work in the television drama *A Man Is Ten Feet Tall* and its film adaptation *Edge of the City* are blueprints for the character work which carried the African American from servant to mythological conscience of a guilty nation. In Robert Alan Arthur's drama, two men—one white and one black—find their lives intertwined to the end when the black man offers shelter to the white army deserter. Christlike, humane, and clearly the model of decency, the black man is killed while defending the white deserter, and dies in his arms.

Clearly, times had changed since the movies where a white, good Samaritan was rewarded with violence and mayhem for taking in a deceptive black man. Even more, television and film producers wanted to exploit the new material for drama opening up on the national scene. Here was fresh blood for audiences eager to distinguish themselves from the conservative generations of the past.

Poitier's role in *Guess Who's Coming To Dinner* (1967) was tailor-made to titillate an audience that was beginning to define itself as progressive, democratic, and anti-war. In *Guess Who's Coming To Dinner*, Poitier plays a black man who is engaged to a white woman. The movie focuses on the tension when she brings him to meet her parents. The couple even share a kiss on-screen, but ever mindful of sponsorship questions, the kiss is rather weakly shown in the rearview mirror of a taxi. Nevertheless, times had changed enough for that contact, brief though it may be, to take place without being accompanied by actual violence.

In similar vein, series television made use of the same dramatic gambits to compel viewers to tune in. *Star Trek's* Nichelle Nichols, who played the Head of Communications Uhura for the starship Enterprise, also shared an on-screen kiss with a white costar. During an episode where Uhura and William Shatner's character Captain Kirk are being held prisoner, they are compelled to kiss against their will. Again, a curious compromise was reached with this watered-down contact. Nichols, too fiery in real life to compromise in her political beliefs, did not pursue acting for many years after the conclusion of *Star Trek*. Instead, in a strange twist of life imitating art, she worked as a recruiter for NASA from the late 1970s until 1987. Dr. Mae Jemison, the first African-American woman astronaut, confessed that she was inspired by Nichols.

There was no doubt about it—African-American actors and actresses were becoming more visible during the 1960s. Networks were looking for ways to attract new and younger viewers without substantially alienating older ones, and ensemble casts that stressed universal brotherhood rather than individual activism seemed the safe way to go. Ratings proved this point. The young,

Clarence Williams III was the hip young African-American undercover cop on *The Mod Squad*, which enthralled audiences with its exciting depiction of life on the streets of Los Angeles.

black star was perceived as "hip," a status mined by the networks on shows like *The Mod Squad* and *Room 222.*

On *Mod Squad*, Clarence Williams III, possessed of a strikingly fashionable Afro and other cool fashions, was supposed to be a recruit to the undercover police force who had been reared in Watts. The Watts riots, a subject of topical interest, were therefore incorporated into the ratings of a television series. As police officers, this young black man and his friends had actually bought into the system, pleasing older viewers, while looking, talking, and acting, for undercover purposes, like counterculture revolutionaries. The combination vaulted the show fairly consistently into the top ten or top twenty in the ratings.

Room 222 was an updated version, in many ways, of Sidney Poitier's *To Sir, With Love* and *The Blackboard Jungle*. A young black teacher struggles with the problems of poverty and the urban experience just enough to qualify the show as liberal. Its appeal, again designed to draw in a broad class of viewers, was based on its heartwarming delivery rather than on its edginess, despite the potential of its subject matter. America wanted to be liberal in the 1960s, but not genuinely frightened.

As a result, stars like Bill Cosby, who returned to the small screen after *I Spy* with a series of his own, found themselves representing African America to the mainstream in gentle and likable formats. Even when the subject matter is difficult—as when Cosby's character, teacher and coach Chester Kincaid, is suspected of being a robbery accomplice because of his color— sitcom standbys prevail: the real suspect turns out to be not just another black man that the police can't tell apart, but Chester's actual double, played also by Bill Cosby.

Cosby's classroom, too, like the starship Enterprise, was a mix of races. Integration, at the close of the 1960s, was beginning to edge out the separate but equal idea that was prevalent at the decade's beginnings on screen. As always, there was a necessity for a comic buffer so that the grittiness of real life was kept from the magical screen. The minstrel show stereotypes, which had a real chance to dissolve in the 1960s, were kept warm by this inability of television to commit itself to much more than escapism. As a result, the 1970s saw a break from the need for African Americans on television to be dignified, and a return to broad comic figures like J. J. on *Good Times* and Huggy Bear on *Starsky and Hutch.*

Comedian Jimmy Walker with a young Janet Jackson on the television series *Good Times.* Walker played a character named J. J. whose silly behavior and "Dy-no-mite!" catchphrase recalled the dandy persona of the minstrel shows of the past. Even other fellow actors complained about the character.

7

A New Generation

In the 1970s, America was newly integrated. Self-consciously, Americans embraced their perceptions of black culture with an avidness that shared no more concern for accuracy than that of their counterparts watching minstrel shows. It may have been a sincere effort at acceptance put forth by many Americans, but in the hands of television networks, blaxploitation reached a zenith in the 1970s. After the turbulent 1960s, African Americans needed to be refitted into a comfortable niche in society. That niche appeared to be sitcoms.

Television series like *Good Times, Sanford and Son,* and *The Jeffersons* professed to celebrate diversity while perpetuating stereotypes familiar from minstrel times. Exaggerated speech and dress, along with shuffling and eye rolling, made a comeback on situation comedy. There were few new Sidney Poitiers or Paul Robesons on series television. Instead, Redd Foxx, as Sanford the junkman, shuffled his wily way through his junk-yard, every now and then rolling his eyes heavenward to assure his dead wife that he was on his way. Despite his autonomy on the show, Sanford was clearly an outcast from the system. His clothes were the ragged overalls of the South, and his diction was folksy.

America took Sanford to heart, joining him in spurning his educated, ironic son LaMont. Crusty, laughable Fred Sanford was a figure from the past that no one wanted his son to modernize. Other television series, quick to capitalize on the instant hipness bestowed by the use of African-American characters, peopled their shows with blacks. However, audiences did not eat up complex and subtle portrayals in the same way they fastened on stock, buffoonish characters, like J. J. on *Good Times*. J. J.'s signature line, "Dy-no-mite!" recalled the phrases of Amos 'n' Andy that America had gleefully repeated thirty years prior. J. J. looked and acted like the dandy of the minstrel show, clothes-conscious yet ridiculous, and a strutting con man.

J. J.'s parents, played by Esther Rolle and John Amos, were well enough delineated and played that they could have been compli-cated and dignified figures despite their appearance in a comedy. But the rollicking performance of Jimmy Walker as J. J. eventually compelled Esther Rolle to discuss her dissatisfaction in *Ebony*: "He's eighteen and he doesn't work. He can't read and write. He doesn't think . . . they have made him more stupid and enlarged the role . . . I resent the imagery." John Amos shared Rolle's opinion, and left after the second season. Rolle quit once after the 1976-1977 season, only to return as the series was dropping in poularity.

What's Happening!!, which appeared first on ABC in 1976 and ran until 1979, revived the wisecracking and overweight domestic figures of bygone days in the person of Mama, a single parent with a bumbling comic son and an equally wisecracking daughter, unkindly labeled by Donald Bogle as "a young servant in waiting."

Just as troubling were the strange combinations of integration represented on television, where a white family would adopt a black child, who was played by an undersized male actor. Both *Diff'rent Strokes* (1978)—and in the '80s, *Webster*—featured this combination. The black child, scheming and clever beyond his seeming years, yet always subject to the final control of his adoptive white father, could have been transported out of any minstrel show which featured black characters asking what they would do if they were left to fend for themselves. The black male actors, whose chronological age did not match their size, invested childhood with disturbingly adult tones, and adulthood with the need for continuing care by a white benefactor.

A slightly higher caliber of comedy was produced by Norman Lear, who created *All In The Family*, a controversial program which challenged racism by its truthful portrayals. Unusual for the "safe" comedy which tended to be broadcast on television, the character of Archie Bunker irascibly exposed the workings of bigotry to a bemused nation. From 1973 to 1975, Sherman Helmsley, Archie Bunker's black counterpart, matched Archie Bunker for racism. Until Helmsley's portrayal of George Jefferson, the matching racism of many members of the African-American community had never found expression on television; it is possible that many Americans had until then been unfamiliar with its depth or resonance. George Jefferson caught the nation's interest with his counter-bigotry, and Helmsley and a talented cast, including Isabel Sanford, "moved on up" to their own series, *The Jeffersons*, in 1974.

The comedy of *The Jeffersons* still depended on George Jefferson strutting like a dandy and trying to con the people around him, but he at least was firmly anchored in marriage with a warm and practical wife who clearly deserved better. His antics were played off against the long-suffering interracial couple next door and his sassy maid, played to the hilt by Marla Gibbs, whose stereotypical performance was rendered pleasingly ironic by the fact that her boss was an African American instead of a white man.

Just as difficult to pigeonhole was the amazing comic talent of Flip Wilson, whose comedy/variety show ran from 1970 to 1974. Flip Wilson created an arsenal of African-American characters, some trite and some not, but he brought an unnerving sarcasm to his eye-rolling which brought his audience to its knees. He pranced

Comedian Flip Wilson (shown here with Tim Conway) dressed as his female character "Geraldine." Wilson's popular show not only won an Emmy award for writing, but also commanded high prices for advertising time and attracted a diverse group of celebrity guest stars.

around, pretending to be a black woman through his alter ego, Geraldine Jones, and a host of other hilarious characters. His versatile body movements and quick wit recalled the minstrel comedy of bygone days for some, but the edge to his work was always apparent. His characters were not safe or neutralized for their appearance on primetime. Wilson, for example, retold the discovery of America to his audience from the perspective of black "Queen Isabel Anderson." This queen sends Columbus to look for Ray Charles, whom she is convinced is in the New World. The West Indians whom Columbus "discovers" irreverently tell him, "We don't wanna be discovered. You better discover your ass away from here."

Stars of various races flocked to perform on the wildly popular show, which ended its run due to Wilson's exhaustion. Lena Horne, Lucille Ball, Diahann Carroll, Bing Crosby, Jack Benny, James Brown, and Stevie Wonder all appeared to the delight of network executives. Wilson and his staff of writers won an Emmy for writing in 1971, and sponsor advertising time became so costly that it was clear that Wilson was "Television's First Black Superstar."

Nevertheless, the intensely private Wilson—who had grown up in a poverty-stricken family with eighteen surviving children and an alcoholic father, as well as living in a series of foster homes—was not an outspoken symbol for civil rights. Instead, he stressed his professionalism, which had included studying the comic craft of Max Eastman. He stated clearly, "I'm selling professional entertainment. Politics is for politicians."

Other black superstars rose to prominence during the 1970s as a new genre of blaxploitation film surfaced. Ultra-hip superhero male stars like Melvin Van Peebles, Richard Roundtree, and Ron O'Neal played militant, angry, ghetto-style black men wreaking "justice" and charming women simultaneously. *Shaft*, *Superfly*, and *Sweet Sweetback's Baad Asssss Song* glamorized the ghetto experience, bringing white America into yet another fake black terrain. Cartoonish images of black male sexuality riddled these flicks, even as they plagued the James Bond series starring a white male from this time period. If there is any lesson to be taken from these images, it is that sexism is just as strong a current as racism.

Billy Dee Williams was a much smoother on-screen lover, appearing in more romantic material such as *Lady Sings the Blues* (1972), a biography of Billie Holiday starring Diana Ross. Williams sold greater sophistication to a swooning female audience in true leading man mode, a foretaste of the devotion to be inspired by later actors like Denzel Washington. Handsome, smooth, and articulate,

Williams refuted the ghetto stereotype as he wooed and won Ross and a host of other leading ladies. He successfully repeated the formula in *Mahogany*, also starring Diana Ross. Ross plays a young woman struggling to leave the ghetto but retain a sense of identity. Williams plays her boyfriend, a politician. As in *Lady Sings the Blues*, melodrama often overtakes the film as the characters attempt to gain part of the American Dream for themselves, generally through buying into the system. Tension develops between the central character's skin color, mahogany, and the success it makes her strain to reach. These movies, which earned Ross and Williams many accolades, spawned a number of copycat films throughout the 1970s.

African Americans in this decade were struggling to be represented on film in characters with professional range. For every Emmy winning performance with a sensitive and complex portrayal of racism, there was a J. J. or Superfly to recall minstrel show stereotypes. African Americans had yet to be represented simply as people with the full range of human emotions, reactions, and potential of mainstream America—until the blockbuster epic *Roots*.

Written by African-American author Alex Haley and starring such luminaries as Cicely Tyson, who had breathed dignified and poignant life into characters in films like *The Autobiography of Miss Jane Pittman* and *Sounder*, *Roots* was nothing short of a phenomenon when it aired in the 1976-1977 television season. *Roots* was a historical docudrama about slavery seen from the point of view of the slaves. Its subject matter was explosive—slavery was not rendered comforting or familiar, nor whitewashed for the benefit of the mainstream audience. Instead, viewers suffered along with characters like Kunta Kinte and Kizzie as they endured degradation and brutality in America under the slave system. Americans were forced to confront the deliberate tearing apart of African families, and the haunting consequences of centuries of rape, separation, torture and humiliation. Above all, the series allowed all Americans to feel African-American pain as it really was—a human pain with no compensation great enough to vindicate the breakdown of

Actors Ben Vereen and Olivia Cole in the landmark television series *Roots*, which unflinchingly examined the trauma of slavery from the viewpoint of the slaves themselves. This series also raised awareness of African-American heritage.

decency. In *Roots*, black Americans were simply human beings and family members. Black heritage became a popular topic of discussion after the advent of *Roots*, and awareness of African-American history rocketed.

Roots proved how powerful a medium television and film could be for social change in the hands of a daring enough and visionary enough filmmaker. Sociological surveys were even conducted in the aftermath of *Roots*, with researchers concluding that the majority of respondents felt "sadness" after viewing such a horrifying segment of American history. The predicted anger and liberalism were secondary to profound sympathy evoked by genuinely human characters. A precedent had been set, but the 1980s did not quite reach the high watermark of *Roots*.

The Cosby Show became one of the most popular television sitcoms ever. Bill Cosby played the patriarch of the Huxtable family, an upper middle-class black family whose trials and tribulations struck a universal chord with viewers. The characters were also refreshingly free of stereotypes.

8

A Changing Vision

Visibility for the African-American performer continued to increase throughout the 1980s with roles in ensemble shows like *Hill Street Blues*; *Trapper John, M.D.*; *L.A. Law*; *WKRP In Cincinnati*; *St. Elsewhere* and *The A-Team*. Black superstars like Eddie Murphy and Richard Pryor began to enjoy stellar success with comic "buddy" movies, and rap—a new genre of music created by African Americans— was making its way onto soundtracks and film. But, despite the greater quantity of work for the black actor or actress, quality roles were few and far between. Then, the phenomenon known as *The Cosby Show* premiered in 1984.

The Cosby Show became the most popular television series of such high quality that had ever aired. The premise was simple. The Huxtables were an upper middle-class family, and the domestic incidents of a household with four (and later five) children provided the basis for the family. For example, one episode might focus on a child's poor grades, or on sibling rivalry, or on the mother's onset of menopause. Bill Cosby, the star of the vehicle, stated, "My one rule is to be true rather than funny." Out of mundane events, small miracles of comedy were created.

Although the family was black, the cultural references were more dignified than stereotyped. The Huxtables were a remarkably well-educated group: Clifford Huxtable, played by Bill Cosby, was a medical doctor, and Clair Huxtable, played by Phylicia Rashad, was a lawyer. The material never deteriorated into raucous insults or antic comedy. There were no overweight domestics, tragic mulattos, dandies, or simpletons. When Clifford's son Theo was revealed to be dyslexic, the series explored the problem with gentle humor and wisdom. No one scored jokes off of Theo because of his reading problem.

The absence of stereotypes was deliberate and carefully monitored. Psychiatrist Alvin Pouissaint, an African American, was hired as a consultant. He monitored every script for negative and stereotypical material, an unprecedented occurrence on network television. He was hired because the show itself was Bill Cosby's vehicle. Cosby was both actor, co-producer, co-creator, and executive consultant. His own comic image and significant earning power were on the line, and he wanted every episode to represent the high quality he had always brought to the screen.

Cosby's vision proved to be very successful. The show appealed to the rising middle class of baby boomers in the United States. It became the number one show on television from 1985 to 1989, drawing 63 million viewers during its most successful phase, generating a 34.9 rating with white audiences and a 48.7 with African-American households. The cost for advertising on the show, always an indicator of prestige, was $380,000 for thirty seconds, according to Donald Bogle.

The Cosby Show ran until the 1991-1992 season, ending with an episode where Theo Huxtable graduated from college. Its spin-off, *A Different World*, was set in college but focused on one Huxtable daughter, Denise, played by Lisa Bonet. *A Different*

World featured a talented cast, many of whom would later rise to prominence—including Sinbad, Marisa Tomei, and Jada Pinkett. Jasmine Guy had a memorable role as the self-absorbed Southern belle, Whitley. As on *The Cosby Show,* the humor evolved from the subtle layers of characterization and gentle reminders of humanity.

Unfortunately, both shows were occasionally charged with "not being Black enough." Despite the fact that Denise's college is all-black, or that the Huxtables wove information about black history like Martin Luther King Jr.'s contributions into the show, some critics charged that the show was "a white family in blackface." Cosby responded with the telling question of why a successful black family should be considered unreal.

The success of the delicately tinged portrayals on *The Cosby Show* influenced the development of other series focused on African Americans, although not to the degree that could be hoped. Frank Reid and Daphne Maxwell Reid, a husband and wife team, also made an attempt to bring a classier depiction of blacks to American television. Their series, *Frank's Place,* was sophisticated and charming, with characters in offbeat roles such as lawyers and funeral directors. The relationship between the husband and wife was the focus of the show, a rarity in black film and television history. The couple displayed a healthy, warm, intelligent relationship around which the show revolved.

The success of this kind of yuppie dramatic comedy opened more roles to African Americans on other television series. Mario Van Peebles—and later, Blair Underwood—played black attorneys on *L.A. Law,* a high-powered show that focused on the crises in a sophisticated and successful law firm. But these roles didn't open doors for more black actors. As Donald Bogle points out, *L.A. Law* "carefully neutralized" the "ethnic background." The real question on the show was whether Reaganomics and its unadulterated capitalist values would entirely engulf the law firm, not a focus on the development of individual characters.

The Cosby Show and its offspring aside, the 1980s was still the era of the ensemble show wherein the African-American character was substantially a one-trick pony. For every Huxtable, there was a Webster or a Mr. T.

Webster seemed like a rerun of *Diff'rent Strokes*, with an under-sized black male adopted by a white family and the sugarcoated result mined for laughter. Revered in Japan for his doll-like stature, Emmanuel Lewis was a cute child whose career did not survive his transition to adulthood. *Webster* attempted to periodically focus on more serious issues such as leukemia and bullying, but the show did not grip the audience with its drama nor break it up with its comedy.

The A-Team, an action-oriented drama, leaned even more towards the cartoonish. All of the characters were affected by the premise—that of a group of soldiers of fortune who were also veterans of Vietnam, traveling the country in order to fight injustice. Mr. T., garishly outfitted with a mohawk hairstyle and layers of gold chains, provided comic muscle to the group. The way he talked and his antic threats were pretty standard for a ghetto tough stereotype, this time used for comedy.

The character of Urkel on the comedy *Family Matters* offered another reinterpretation of antic comedy. It was a popular series which ran from 1989 to 1998. Urkel was simply a buffoon (though a good-hearted one) for much of the show's run, with enough eye-rolling, physically antic, shuffling, comic distortions to recall the stereotypes of a minstrel show. In the talented hands of actor Jaleel White, however, the character of Urkel moved ever so subtly to draw the audience's sympathy by the last few seasons of the show.

The 1980s saw the rise of black comic actors on the big screen reaching unprecedented heights. Eddie Murphy, Danny Glover, and Richard Pryor, each teamed with a white actor, demonstrated that a new formula—the interracial "buddy" movie with heavy doses of action and of comedy—could grab audience attention and generate blockbuster earnings. The success of the buddy movies on film led to the phenomenally successful pairing of Crockett and Tubbs on television's *Miami Vice.*

Richard Pryor and Gene Wilder teamed up for a series of buddy movies. *Silver Streak*, which came out in 1976, was highly successful, and set the formula for future buddy movies that paired two unlikely partners of different races.

Richard Pryor led the pack. He stamped the old minstrel show standby of antic comedian with his own personal and compelling brand of craziness. He spoke in dialect, like the old performers who had so intrigued mainstream audiences, and affected a wild, playful, and even sexy character that audiences loved. In the 1960s and 1970s, he starred in an array of films, like *The Busy Body* (1967), *Wild In The Streets* (1968), *The Green Berets, The Phynx* (1970), *You've Got To Walk It Like You Talk It Or You'll Lose That*

Beat (1971), *Dynamite Chicken* (1972), *Wattstax* (1973), *Hit!* (1973), *The Mack, Some Call It Loving* (1973), *Uptown Saturday Night, Let's Do It Again, The Bingo Long Traveling All-Stars and Motor Kings*, and *Car Wash*. He also appeared in less comic fare such as *Lady Sings the Blues*.

Then Pryor teamed up with white comic actor Gene Wilder for the smash hit *Silver Streak* (1976). Audiences ate up this pairing, literally falling out of their movie seats laughing as the two played off of each other. The magic carried him through less successful undertakings following *Silver Streak*, such as *Greased Lightning, Which Way Is Up?, Blue Collar* (1978), and *California Suite* (1978). He also did a turn in the largely children's productions of *The Wiz* (1978) and *The Muppet Movie* (1979). But he did not hit his stride again until he returned to his stand-up comedy roots in *Richard Pryor Live In Concert* (1979). Unfortunately, Pryor's personal life and health problems resulted in his eventual withdrawal from the screen.

Eddie Murphy, Danny Glover, and Gregory Hines drew on Pryor's example and crafted successful performances in "buddy" movies which recalled *Silver Streak* throughout the eighties. Their outings all included hefty doses of comedy within the framework of action pictures, a formula that is still going strong.

Eddie Murphy starred in the enormously popular *48 Hrs.* with Nick Nolte. The hardcore banter between Murphy's character, a convict released into the custody of Nolte's policeman in order to locate a killer, intrigued audiences. Racism is tackled head on as Nolte's character learns to work with Murphy's. In telling dialogue from the film, for example, a superficially reformed Murphy refers to himself in a bar as the nightmare of America— a "negro with a badge."

Murphy parlayed his success into international stardom with his roles in the *Beverly Hills Cop* movies. In the 1984 film, which spawned two sequels, the racism question is again mined for laughs as Murphy is cast as a black cop from Detroit with street mannerisms who is then transplanted into Beverly Hills to find a killer. Much of the humor derives from the clash of perspectives—again a minstrel show image in many ways. The formula was so successful that the follow-up appeared in 1987.

The buddy idea also animated the *Lethal Weapon* series, starring Danny Glover and white heartthrob Mel Gibson. Gibson, however, played the suicidal and antic comic in this pairing, while Glover was a middle-class and likable family man who serves as a straight man to some of the funniest scenes in movie history. For example, Glover's character is forced by a bomb to remain on the toilet while Gibson's character works to free him. Audiences loved this unsophisticated fare. 1986's *Running Scared*, starring Gregory Hines and Billy Crystal, also followed the same lines. The two actors, one white and one black, were partners, and the comedy was as important as the action.

Oddly enough, the pairings on television rather than on the big screen were more successful when they focused on action instead. *Ten Speed and Brownshoe*, a pairing of detectives which hinged on comedy, failed to ignite viewers' interest, but a phenomenon called *Miami Vice* had an enormous impact on pop culture of the 1980s.

In 1984, *Miami Vice* debuted. It starred stylishly hip cops in a fantasy setting of pastels and art deco architecture–otherwise known as Miami, Florida. Donald Bogle says that the concept for the show was basically "MTV Cops." Aimed at a generation seeking style over substance, the clothing of cops Crockett and Tubbs was as important an issue as the plot, which usually included a selection of Miami's drug underworld, occasionally portrayed by such music stars as Glenn Frey of the Eagles. Good-looking actors Phillip Michael Thomas and Don Johnson quickly became stars on a show which at first seemd like an ensemble. The soundtrack was a veritable who's who of MTV hits, with U2, Phil Collins, Run-DMC, Chaka Khan, Lionel Richie, Tina Turner, and Cyndi Lauper, reminding the viewer repeatedly just how hip and slick the show was. The show was violent and the lead actors handsome and brooding. *Miami Vice*

Miami Vice was a hugely successful television show that starred Don Johnson and Phillip Michael Thomas as cops dealing with Miami's criminal underworld.

proved immensely popular, drawing enormous ratings every Friday night and inspiring fashion trends.

1980s audiences liked seeing the black male in an action role, a great reversal from the dawn of the celluloid era and a measure of changing perspectives. A standout performance by Louis Gossett Jr. in 1982's *An Officer and a Gentleman* opposite

Richard Gere earned Gossett the third Oscar ever won by a black actor in a supporting role. The playing field may not have been leveled, but at least there were black actors and actresses negotiating it. Some, like Eddie Murphy, were so successful that their earnings marked them as superstars, as they were capable of opening a picture and pulling in millions of viewers. Comic superstars like Murphy were paid substantially better than the average, too.

And so were nurturing black figures on television, if talk show salaries were anything to go by. The best-paid figure on television may eventually prove to be Oprah Winfrey, the savvy talk show hostess who parlayed a film career in movies like *The Color Purple*, directed by Steven Spielberg and co-starring Whoopi Goldberg, into a talk show empire. Winfrey's shrewd financial dealings have made her one of the power brokers of the small screen, and her daily doses of advice and comfort to viewers have created a powerful legacy with a host of imitators. Few can rival her ability to interview stars or to elevate authors to best-selling status.

Her longevity is also remarkable in a profession where celebrities, like fashions, come and go quickly. Her influence extended throughout the 1990s, and Oprah still wields great power over television. She has always used it to open doors for others to follow. Slowly but surely, the face of the African American on television and film is changing.

Marlon Wayans, Keenan Ivory Wayans and Shawn Wayans at the premiere of *Scary Movie 2*. Their television show *In Living Color* was highly successful, providing a fresh urban spin on sketch comedy, and launched the careers of many of its actors, including Damon Wayans, David Alan Grier, Jamie Foxx and Jim Carrey.

9

Leading Roles

The 1990s and the dawn of the twenty-first century was a more eclectic time for African Americans on-screen than any other. All-black situation comedy shows proliferated, as did talk shows, ensemble dramas, and movies depicting "the 'hood," giving black actors and actresses a wider pool of images to explore. But, compared to the numbers of African-American viewers and the number of roles overall available, African-American performers even in the 1990s remained largely invisible with the exception of a few standouts. The NAACP and other civil rights organizations lambasted the lack of blacks behind the camera as well as in front of it, as equal representation can only be achieved with equal power behind the scenes.

In the 1990s, more African-American actors, following the model of Bill Cosby a decade earlier, demanded a hand in crafting and displaying their work. The Wayans brothers, for example, used the success of their comedy/variety show *In Living Color* as a springboard to other starring vehicles. *In Living Color* was a fresh update of 1960s formats like *Laugh-In* and the perennial hit *Saturday Night Live,* featuring the "Fly Girls," who recalled Solid Gold Dancers from music shows, and playing off of stereotypes of black neighborhoods for such regular material as the Homey the Clown and the "Homeboy Shopping Network." *In Living Color* was hip and funny. It launched white comic genius Jim Carrey, as well as vaulting the Wayans brothers to household names.

Some stars became breakouts. They crafted personas, like Wesley Snipes, to represent themselves on screen, much as John Wayne and Clint Eastwood had done decades earlier. These personae were honed to a sharper and sharper edge until they were the essence of cool and hardcore. In 1992, Snipes hit the big time after a series of smaller films. *Passenger 57,* starring Snipes as anti-terrorist expert named John Cutter, is traveling on a plane which is hijacked by insanely violent Charles Rane, played by Bruce Payne. Also featuring Elizabeth Hurley as a psychotic stewardess who is a confederate of Rane, this violent and fast-paced movie inspired audiences with its two-dimensional fight of good versus evil, much like Bruce Willis' *Die Hard.* America was at war, and was seeking an affirmation of uniquely American strength.

Snipes went on to make other successful films, including *Water Dance,* a feature with Woody Harrelson called *White Men Can't Jump,* and the stylish but gory vampire outing *Blade.* Interestingly, Snipes is a gifted comedian but is better received in his silent and menacing big-screen characters. At the beginning of the film era, such portrayals would have been cause for lynching. The journey of African-American performers has been long and is not finished, but certainly there has been change.

The career of Will Smith argues persuasively that a better era is possible. Will Smith, who began as a relatively non-threatening rapper (in comparison to other more violent "gangsta" contemporaries) under the moniker The Fresh Prince and performing with DJ Jazzy Jeff, turned his rising fame as a musician into a television role. He played the part of a boy from the 'hood who moves in with his relatives in Beverly Hills. Showing great promise as a comic actor, the series skyrocketed with Smith gradually dominating every episode.

Smith's career really took off when he demonstrated his universal appeal as a leading man in the 1990s blockbuster *Independence Day*, where he literally plays a great role in saving the entire human race from marauding aliens. He did it with enough boyish charm to dispel violent stereotypes, and enough bravado to come across as a solid American hero. People began to sit up and take notice of Smith's ability to carry a picture.

Another stylish and charming African-American leading man transfixed American audiences late in the 1980s: Denzel Washington. Washington has received a total of five Oscar nominations—a number astonishing for any performer, let alone an African American in a mainstream industry. He was nominated for *Cry Freedom* (1987), *Glory* (1989), *Malcolm X* (1992), *The Hurricane* (1999), and *Training Day* (2001). He won the Best Supporting Actor Oscar in 1989 for *Glory*.

In 1993 an African-American actress broke Oscar ground with her 1993 Oscar nomination for *What's Love Got To Do With It*, a film based on the autobiography of rock superstar Tina Turner. Angela Bassett's nomination was all the more amazing considering that up until her amazing and multidimensional turn as a leading lady, she had only played smaller roles in a handful of movies. She can be seen in *F/X* (1986), *Kindergarten Cop* (1990), *City of Hope* (1991), and *Passion Fish* (1992). She had larger roles in 1991's *Boyz N The Hood* opposite Laurence Fishburne and in *Malcolm X*, which starred Denzel Washington.

But the landscape for African-American performers in the 1990s had still not reached its potential. NAACP President Kwesi Mfume noted that only 19 nonwhites—including Asians, Latinos, Native Americans, and African Americans— had even been included in any of the top award categories from 1990 to 1999. There were a few faces that were both

Angela Bassett received an Oscar nomination for her portrayal of Tina Turner in the movie *What's Love Got To Do With It*. Although she didn't win, it was a monumental achievement in itself and for her career, which skyrocketed after her nomination.

familiar and up-and-coming, such as Whoopi Goldberg and Cuba Gooding Jr., but the numbers were not what they should be. Controversy had given way to invisibility, as complacent Americans imagined the civil rights struggle had been successfully resolved.

Meanwhile, the movies that continued to pull in viewers and create box office dollars were not always of the highest quality. But what American film audiences were eager for in the 1990s was the kind of film that delivered a gritty urban perspective, with its black stars prepared for any kind of violence. In 1991, nineteen films by black directors awaited release. The four that had the greatest impact were similar in theme: *Boys N The Hood, Jungle Fever, Straight Out of Brooklyn,* and *New Jack City.* They explored the process of forming an identity in a pressured urban environment.

The four combined generated about $165 million. *Boys N The Hood* accounted for $45.4 million alone. It became a new cultural icon. *In Living Color* satirically rode the wave of "Hood" movies claiming to be gritty tales of urban reality, but there was no questioning this genre's immense popularity. White and non-white American youth, drawn by the lyrics of rap and hip-hop music to what they saw as an exciting and hip underbelly to urban America, flocked to these menacing and often spiritually empty movies about the African-American experience with poverty and gangs. Musicians like Tupac Shakur, LL Cool J, Janet Jackson and Queen Latifah crossed disciplines in order to star in these films, which offered up a corrective to the Cosby vision of a black middle class. America itself was fighting a wave of unemployment, crime, and a war in the Persian Gulf, and during the 1990s the movie screen reflected urban disillusionment. Ice-T and Ice Cube, as well as rapper Will Smith, rose to prominence in all black vehicles that convinced a nation, like minstrel shows once had, that they were getting an authentic experience of black culture.

Boyz N The Hood opened with a sobering message—that one out of every twenty one African-American males dies before reaching adulthood. The greatest portion are killed by another black male. This terrifying and exceedingly dramatic statistic overshadowed most depictions of the on-screen African American in the 1990s. It also provided a good excuse to virtually ignore the experience of black women when it came to creating subject matter for films.

Black women remained more visible on the small screen, however, in stock situation comedies like *Living Single* or as talk show hostesses like Oprah or her smaller-scale imitators. Often a singer would appear as an actress, or an actress would perform as a talk show host or in a nightclub. In order to find work, black actresses have long been more versatile than their mainstream peers.

Like Eartha Kitt decades earlier, actress and nightclub singer Della Reese is a case in point. Della Reese has been a performer of one sort or another for more than five decades. By the time she was thirteen, young Della (then Deloreese Patricia Early) was singing with gospel superstar Mahalia Jackson. She had a hit of her own with "Don't You Know," but her career did not accelerate until she appeared on *The Ed Sullivan Show.*

She was to do many guest appearances on variety shows, including *The Mike Douglas Show.* She spent much of her time doing shows in Las Vegas. Ironically, like many African-American performers before her, she was disallowed to go in the casino or sleep in any of the hotels in which she performed. Ed Sullivan himself was distressed by the situation, and often intervened.

Then, the era of the nightclub came and went. Reese found herself, like other African-American entertainers, searching for venues in which to perform. She settled upon acting. Television series like *The Mod Squad* featured her in the late 1960s. She followed that with more work, appearing as a regular on such 1970s fare as *Chico and the Man, It Takes Two, Charlie & Co.,* and *The Royal Family.* In the 1980s, she worked on *Designing Women, L.A. Law,* and *Night Court.* Finally in the 1990s, she began playing the role she currently holds on-screen, that of the undercover angel Tess on *Touched By An Angel,* which also stars Roma Downey. Reese's character is both sharp-tongued and nurturing, a role instantly recognizable from years of African-American film history.

Most African-American actresses and actors employed in the last decade of the twentieth century were cast members of ensemble shows, like *ER* and *Law and Order,* or played non-major roles in soap operas. Few experienced the instant recognition of Della Reese or Bill Cosby, particularly black female performers. However, television has been particularly kind to Queen Latifah. Queen Latifah, whose real name is Dana Owens,

Queen Latifah started as a rapper, but soon became a film and television actor, appearing in movies like *Jungle Fever* and *Set It Off*, and the sitcom *Living Single*. She also began hosting her own daytime talk show.

is the daughter of a policeman and a high school teacher in her native New Jersey. She renamed herself in high school, and formed her own rap group. Several odd jobs later, including a stint at Burger King, she gained a record contract and began making smash hip-hop albums. Her 1989 album, *All Hail The Queen*, and her later success, *Black Reign*, established her solidly on the music scene. Women in droves identified with Queen Latifah's songs like "The Evil That Men Do" and "Ladies First."

Queen Latifah also rode the crest of the early '90s movies glamorizing the grittiness of the urban African-American experience. She acted in Spike Lee's *Jungle Fever* and in *House Party 2*, a silly but hip comedy. With those acting credentials under her belt, she turned to television.

Fox television found a perfect vehicle for her. *Living Single* was a situation comedy about the lives of a group of young African-American women. They were all represented as professionals, although the sitcom was rife with many of the usual stereotypes. For example, one of the women was always looking for a rich husband. Critics charged that all the women did, really, was talk about men. However, it was no better nor worse than any other sitcom that did not star African Americans, and the comedy formulas themselves were long known to make the networks money. Queen Latifah played Khadijah, who emerged as a comfortable and independent character who edited a hip magazine called *Flavor*. Queen Latifah's imposing presence brought in many viewers. Nearly six feet tall and favoring dress which included an African-style turban, she was openly proud of her African heritage and of her own power and assertiveness. Female viewers loved her.

Other family-oriented comedies arose in the wake of the quintessential family show *The Cosby Show*. Currently on television, viewers can watch *Moesha,* about a young black woman and her family. Starring Brandy, who is also an R&B singer, the show capitalized upon her emotive abilities and wholesome image for the half-hour situation comedy. Damon Wayans drew on the success of *The Cosby Show* to construct the current hit *My Wife and Kids.* Wayans is the driving force behind the series, which is the only major network African-American sitcom to draw in large numbers of white audience members. Wayans attributes this popularity to the fact the *My Wife and Kids,* like *The Cosby Show,* deliberately "neutralizes" race questions. The comedy is intrinsic to the family situation, and the father is a universal figure who is too smart for his kids to run rings around him. Wayans himself explains, "The stories have a definite universality, and the main theme is 'I'm not your friend. I'm your dad, and I'll be your dad until I die.' It's about a father being a disciplinarian."

Wayans' own character is a professional who owns his own delivery truck company. He is successful enough that he gets to spend a good deal of time at home with his own children. His wife, played by Tisha Campbell-Martin, is a part-time stockbroker. Their three kids include two teenagers and a five-year-old. Like *The Cosby Show,* the humor is generated through family interaction, not insulting or antic violence. The Screen Actors Guild Commission Report states that, in general, African Americans are ghettoized on television; Wayans' comedy, however, successfully avoids that trap.

Some 12 million viewers weekly tune in to Wayans' show. Neema Barnett, a visiting Film Professor at UCLA's School of Theater, Film, and Television, relates that success to the success of *The Cosby Show,* saying, "There is a clear similarity. Both are about slices of life that everyone can relate to. They give the American public the chance to see black people just as people."

Actor Campbell-Martin concurs. "We don't focus on black or white," she says. "Damon works so hard at delivering lessons without hitting people over the head." Wayans' positive messages about parenting are obviously appreciated by a large segment of Americans, be they African American or not.

Some of the other networks, such as UPN and the WB, are encouraged by these successes and rely on black-centered programming. Black interviewers and talk show hosts, like the perennially hip Arsenio Hall, the stately journalist Ed Bradley, the polished host Bryant Gumbel, and the upright and charismatic Montel Williams, have become daily visitors in American homes. The stand-up comedy talents of Steve Harvey and Bernie Mac have also led to the creation of television vehicles starring them as the beleaguered but professionally successful heads of all-black households. The networks have always preferred to take risks on proven comedians and performers.

Unfortunately, not every one of these series is of high quality. Racism was played for laughs—and to little audience appeal—in *The Hughleys,* starring comedian D.L. Hughley, in what often seemed a reenactment of George Jefferson. And the sexism that was more muted in *Living Single* was fairly direct in the sitcom *Martin,* a showcase for black comedian Martin Lawrence. Martin Lawrence got his big break from a 1987 appearance on *Star Search.* After that, he appeared in various television series and movies like *What's Happening Now!!* (a follow-up series to *What's Happening!!*), *House Party,* Spike Lee's *Do The Right Thing,* and *Boomerang.* But it was his openly raunchy stand-up comedy performances that developed his reputation as a performer. His slapsticky antics and sexism were mined for laugh after laugh, but critics charge that this voice of the hip-hop generation turned black women into degraded objects for the delight of a less than sensitive viewing audience. Martin's relationship with his girlfriend (and eventual wife) Gina was plagued with descents into a battle for power between the sexes; no healthy, *Cosby*-style relationship was modeled for the surprisingly large viewing audience. Nevertheless, Lawrence's films, such as *Big Momma's House,* have proven very popular.

Women simply did not figure at all into the blockbuster film made by Chris Tucker with Asian action star Jackie Chan. The *Rush Hour* formula, with heavy, slapsticky, entirely inarticulate comedy, scored big in America and overseas. Another successful "buddy" outing, women were no more than objects in the film, a charge that truthfully can be levelled at the majority of action movies, whomever they starred. In 2001, a slightly meatier role in *Romeo Must Die* was played by the late Aaliyah opposite Jet Li, but his high-kicking martial arts were clearly the centerpiece.

African-American women deserved more respect than they received on screen in the last decade. Although enormous change had occurred since the advent of the film, radio, and television industry, a level playing field still did not exist. Then, an amazing event took place at the Academy Awards in 2002.

Jackie Chan and Chris Tucker put their own spin on the classic buddy movie formula with their popular *Rush Hour* movies, throwing together an Asian martial artist and an African-American cop, with predictable hilarity ensuing.

Halle Berry and Denzel Washington celebrate their historic Oscar wins at the 2002 Academy Awards. Berry won Best Actress for *Monster's Ball* and Washington won Best Actor for *Training Day*.

10

New Icons

The image of on-screen African Americans at the beginning of the twenty-first century had changed considerably since its roots in the minstrel shows of nineteenth-century America. However, genuine equality had still not been achieved either on television or film. African-American performers engineering careers in the entertainment industry are well aware of the prejudices, direct and indirect, which continue to challenge non-whites. Some, like Sheila Frazier, assistant director of network talent at Black Entertainment Television, felt discouraged enough to try and create for themselves an alternative to acting that would also serve to employ other African Americans.

Then, for the first time in the history of the Oscar, the awards for both Best Actor and Best Actress went to African Americans. Halle Berry won for her role in *Monster's Ball*, and Denzel Washington accepted his second Oscar for *Training Day*. Seventy-four years of Academy Awards had never seen such an event.

Halle Berry cried openly as she accepted her award, and her acceptance speech highlighted the struggle faced by all performers of color as she said, "This moment is so much bigger than me. This moment is for Dorothy Dandridge, Lena Horne, Diahann Carroll. It's for the women who stand beside me, Jada Pinkett, Angela Bassett, Viveca Fox, and the nameless, faceless women of color who now stand a chance tonight because the door has been opened."

Denzel Washington stressed his connection to Sidney Poitier, recipient of the Board of Governors honor for lifetime achievement and the only African-American actor to that point to have won a Best Actor Oscar. He said, "I'm already a part of history in so many ways. I am just glad to know Sidney Poitier. I just feel closer to him now."

Washington is no stranger to the Academy Awards. Nominated five times, he won the Best Supporting Actor Oscar for *Glory* twelve years previously. His highly acclaimed performance in 1999's *The Hurricane* left many surprised that he had not taken that Oscar too, although his competition was fierce. In reality, only nine percent of non-white nominees have ever made it to the nominations for the top five awards. Washington has long been breaking the mold.

Halle Berry, too, has had a long struggle to be recognized as anything but a beautiful woman. Her breakthrough roles, as far as critical acclaim determine, came with Spike Lee's 1991 *Jungle Fever*, where she demonstrated her abilities playing a homeless crack addict. She further deglamorized herself playing an addict fighting to retain her son's custody in *Losing Isaiah*. Finally, in the year 2000, she won a Golden Globe for her performance on an HBO biography as Dorothy Dandridge, to whom she paid tribute in her Oscar acceptance speech.

The impact of these awards is difficult to determine. For some, the wins are inspiring. Sheila Frazier, for example, said, "I am inspired to act again." As a result of the Academy Awards, she decided to have five hundred of her head shots reproduced, and begin again the search for work as an African-American actress. She says that if the Academy Awards taught her anything, it's "just do it."

Others are less convinced that the awards are more than a single beautiful moment, and that no further change is signified by the strong showing of African Americans at the 2001 Oscars—which, incidentally, included the evening's hostess, comedienne Whoopi Goldberg. Todd Boyd, Professor of Critical Studies at the University of Southern California School of Cinema Television, is taking a wait-and-see attitude. *The Los Angeles Times* quotes Boyd's voice of reason: "Only time will tell if these awards result in concrete changes for the industry as a whole." He adds, "We are way premature in potentially celebrating these victories as some watershed event in Hollywood." Even *Monster's Ball* producer Lee Daniels expresses some reservations about the impact the award will have on Halle's career, which now will be closely watched as an indicator of African-American status in Hollywood. Daniels says, "I sometimes wonder if the Oscar is the kiss of death, actually."

He adds, however, that no one really knows what the result will be, saying, "With Halle we are looking at a different situation because she's black and it's a first—we are treading new water here." Others point out the unfairness of settling the progress of an entire group of people on the shoulders of one or two performers. Screenwriter Cheryl Edwards debates how correct it is to chart the careers of all African Americans using one as a yardstick. She states that Denzel Washington should just be considered a fine performer, but that he should not now be regarded as the "great black hope."

Audiences themselves now chime in with their own views of the debate concerning the significance of the Oscars. Interviews in the African-American community, according to *The Los Angeles Times* staff writer Carla Hall, demonstrate the deep-seated bitterness and doubt the African-American viewing audience has concerning fair representation.

At the very least, there is no consensus. One of the interviewees felt that Berry was honored because she was in a "derogatory" role; another thought that Washington won because Russell Crowe, a white performer considered a shoe-in for Best Actor for his performance in *A Beautiful Mind*, had acted up too much before the awards. Washington's win, therefore, was just "a token thing." Others did not agree. Kevin Boyd, who works as a television writer, did not feel that Crowe's performance was better than Washington's, and that credit was deserved by Washington.

One thing is for certain: the doubts about the status of the African-American performer in the entertainment industry continue, even with such a spectacular proof that some things *have* changed. Maybe the worst legacy of racism on screen will be the Catch-22 of determining progress, where winning an award inspires as much criticism of the industry as losing it. True equality lies in the freedom not to pigeonhole, as John McWhorter so aptly points out in a 2001 article in *The New Republic*. McWhorter, a professor of linguistics at the University of California at Berkeley, is also the author of *Losing the Race: Self Sabotage in Black America*. He reviews the work of Donald Bogle, who has pinpointed the presence of demeaning stereotypes in the entertainment industry in the past century, but presents an interesting case for allowing African Americans to hope for progress.

McWhorter writes that although he does not wish "to suggest that there is no basis for an anxiety about stereotypes," he thinks that the search itself for stereotypes may also be a problem in the advancement of a people. He questions why the issue of stereotypes is given so much importance, given that "it presumes that anything short of a 'sensitive' and 'honest' depiction of black experience constitutes an obstacle to advancement." Very few roles on screen, for blacks or for whites, constitute a sensitive and honest depiction, and ultimately the viewer should be encouraged to understand that television does not represent reality. His final, important concern is that "no form of entertainment has ever achieved such representational justice, and the implication that black Americans are helpless without it renders us passive victims rather than masters of our own fates."

However, McWhorter's sophisticated understanding of popular entertainment may not answer the question of an African-American child or adult seeking tools with which to form an identity or to develop a sense of importance in mainstream American culture. The entertainment industry undoubtedly sends powerful images to the majority of the country, despite the unreality of the screen. There is certainly some cause for worry still. As a sociologist, Dr. Darnell Hunt, the Director of African American Studies at the University of Southern California, comments, "The ways in which groups are included on or excluded from America's dominant medium reflect, in strikingly visual terms, unresolved questions about power imbalances in our society."

Equality has not been achieved by the entertainment industry in America. The Screen Actors Guild report for 1999 states explicitly that Africans Americans on television are still segregated by network, by show type, and even by the night of the week they are broadcast.

"The African American Television Report," conducted by Dr. Hunt, examined 380 episodes of 87 prime time series on ABC, CBS, NBC, FOX, UPN, and WB. Slightly half of all blacks on television are on situation comedies, compared to only a third of all white characters. Most African-American screen regulars appear for less than a minute, and are not representative of their show's main story line. Monday and Friday night are "black" nights on television compared to other times, accounting for more than half of all of the on-screen African Americans per week. The days of Oscar Micheaux and his Midnight Theatre, aimed at all black audiences, suddenly don't seem so distant. (It should be noted that two networks, UPN and WB, are better at featuring African Americans in primetime than their competition.) Images of black achievement broadcast logically have an impact on the continuation of prejudice in America. If this is a "gross misunderstanding"

Sidney Poitier, the first (and for a while, only) African-American actor to receive the Best Actor Oscar, was all too aware of the history made by the Oscar wins of Denzel Washington and Halle Berry. Here Poitier is shown in a scene from his 1963 film *Lilies of the Field*, for which he won his Best Actor Oscar.

of popular entertainment, as McWhorter suggests, it may be one shared by too many people to disregard.

Americans are more likely to be influenced by the drama of Berry's win, drawn into her eloquence and emotion as she whispered, "It's taken seventy-four years to get here. I've got to take this time," before she calmed down enough to accept her hard-won honor. Denzel Washington, graceful as always, acknowledged his debt to the performers who came before, also presenting a powerful image of the importance of African-American predecessors on film: "Forty years I've been chasing Sidney

[Poitier], and they give it to me the same night. I'll always be chasing you, and there's nothing I'd rather do."

The venerable Sidney Poitier himself offered up this analysis of change in the image of on-screen African Americans, both on television and in films. He commented, "Things have changed, clearly. If you came to this venue tonight and saw the array of minority actors headed by some extraordinary people, then you know that things have changed. I think it's a question of degree. To speak of Hollywood as if there has not been change is not fair."

But, he adds, "You can question the speed of it and question whether it will last."

His comments are a testament to the times in which he has lived, spanning the better part of the twentieth century. His trust in the mainstream entertainment industry is guarded and measured by that lifetime of experience which have made him an icon to other African-American actors and actresses like Denzel Washington and Halle Berry.

Berry adds, however, that Poitier is "not just an African-American treasure, he's an American treasure." Perhaps true equality finally lies in just such observations.

1822   English actor Charles Matthews performs the first minstrel show in blackface in Great Britain, based on songs and dances he observed during a trip to the United States. The show is titled *A Trip to America*.

1828   Thomas Dartmouth "Daddy" Rice popularizes the blackface minstrel in America. He performs a caricature of a crippled plantation slave in a song and dance routine who sings a song called "Jump Jim Crow."

1836   The Jim Crow character is such a popular routine that it becomes a standard character portrayed in most minstrel shows performed by a variety of actors.

1910   Theater and film pioneer Sigmund Lubin produced the Rastus and Sambo comedy short film series. These films, starting with *Rastus in Zululand* and *How Rastus Gets His Turkey* (both released in 1910), depicted blacks as unintelligent clowns. All the actors were whites in blackface makeup.

1914   Sam Lucas is the first African-American actor to star in a film. He plays the role of Uncle Tom in Harriet Beecher Stowe's *Uncle Tom's Cabin* (in previous versions this role was played by a white actor).

1920   Nina Mae McKinney stars in *Hallelujah*, her first major role and Hollywood's most important all-black film of that time. McKinney was the first black actor to be recognized as a potential mainstream star.

1925   Paul Robeson, legendary stage actor and scholar, makes his film acting debut in Oscar Micheaux's *Body and Soul*.

1929   Stepin Fetchit is discovered in *Hearts of Dixie*, the first all-black cast musical. He would become the first black Hollywood star and one of the most controversial comedians of his time.

1930   Willie Best appears in his first feature *Ladies of Leisure*. He was typecast as half-awake, dimwitted characters for over twenty years, and his acting style was frequently criticized. He would go on to popularize a character named "Sleep N' Eat."

1934   Louise Beavers appears in her breakthrough performance in the film *Imitation of Life*. Her career would span three decades, during which she would play a series of domestic servant roles.

1939 Hattie McDaniel becomes the first African-American actor to win an Oscar, winning the Best Supporting Actress category for *Gone With the Wind*.

1943 Lena Horne plays her first leading roles in *Cabin in the Sky* and *Stormy Weather*. She is the first African American in Hollywood to be glamorized and publicized by her studio.

1950 Ethel Waters plays the title role in the television series *Beulah*. Her career included a successful stint as a singer and actress on the nightclub circuit and Broadway. She was nominated for her role as Best Supporting Actress for the film *Pinky* in 1949.

1951 Spencer Williams stars as "Andy" in the controversial television show *Amos 'n' Andy*. He made a name for himself as a writer director during the '30s and '40s. However it would be his leading role in *Amos 'n' Andy* for which he would be most remembered.

1954 Dorothy Dandridge stars in *Carmen Jones*, which garnered her an Academy Award nomination in the Best Actress category.

1963 Sidney Poitier stars in the film *Lilies of the Field*. He becomes the first African-American actor to win an Oscar in the Best Actor category for the film.

1968 Diahann Carroll stars in *Julia*, which makes television history by casting her in a role as an educated and widowed mother. It would mark the first time that a series featured a black woman who was not a domestic servant.

1973 Pam Grier stars in *Coffy*, becoming an action movie leading lady in such films as *Sheba, Baby, Foxy Brown* and others. Because of her assertive, tough-girl heroine roles, she was featured on the cover of *Ms.*, though many critics dismissed her as a viable screen personality.

1982 Eddie Murphy stars in *48 Hrs.*, making a career switch from television to film. A year later he stars in *Trading Places*, but his role in the 1984 blockbuster *Beverly Hills Cop* would afford him superstar status.

1986 Whoopi Goldberg stars in *Jumpin' Jack Flash*—the first time an African-American woman comedian would star in a Hollywood comedy. She was nominated for an Academy Award in the Best Actress category for her debut role in *The Color Purple* in 1985, and would win for Best Supporting Actress for *Ghost* in 1990.

1987 Denzel Washington receives his first Oscar nomination for *Cry Freedom.* In 1989 he would win for Best Supporting Actor for *Glory,* and then earn nominatinos for Best Actor for *Malcolm X* in 1992 and *The Hurricane* in 1999.

1989 Will Smith, the first of a number of successful rap artists that would take their careers to the big and small screen, stars in the television sitcom *The Fresh Prince of Bel Air.* As the show grows in popularity he expands to film. Other hip-hop stars following his lead include LL Cool J, Ice-T, Ice Cube, Queen Latifah and others.

1996 Cuba Gooding Jr. wins the Oscar in the Best Supporting Actor category for his portrayal of a football star in *Jerry Maguire.*

2002 Will Smith receives his first Oscar nomination for his role in the film *Ali.* Both Halle Berry (*Monster's Ball*) and Denzel Washington (*Training Day*) win in the Best Actress and Best Actor categories, respectively. Sidney Poitier is honored with a Lifetime Achievement Award.

Bogle, Donald. *Primetime Blues: African Americans on Network Television.*
New York: Farrar, Straus & Giroux, 2001.

Cripps, Thomas. *Slow Fade to Black: The Negro in American Film 1900-1942.*
New York: Oxford University Press, 1977.

Guerrero, Ed. *Framing Blackness: the African American Image in Film.*
Philadelphia: Temple University Press, 1993.

Julliard, Ahrgus. Bart, Andrews, *Holy Mackerel: The Amos N' Andy Story.*
New York: E. P. Dutton, 1986.

Mapp, Edward. *Blacks in American Films: Today and Yesterday.* Metuchen,
New Jersey: Scarecrow Press, 1972.

Null, Gary. *Black Hollywood: the Negro in Motion Pictures.* Secaucus,
New Jersey: Citadel Press, 1975.

Bergman, Carol. *Sidney Poitier.* Los Angeles, CA: Melrose Square Publishing, 1990.

De Angelis, Theresa. *Denzel Washington.* New York and Philadelphia: Chelsea House Publishers, 1998.

Fitzgerald, Dawn, *Angela Bassett.* New York and Philadelphia: Chelsea House Publishers, 2001.

Herbert, Solomon J., *Bill Cosby.* New York and Philadelphia: Chelsea House Publishers, 1992.

Naden, Corinne J. and Rose Blue, *Halle Berry.* New York and Philadelphia: Chelsea House Publishers, 2001.

Larsen, Rebecca, *Paul Robeson.* New York: Franklin Watts Publishing, 1989.

Palmer, Leslie, *Lena Horne,* New York and Philadelphia: Chelsea House Publishers, 1989.

Stauffer, Stacy, *Will Smith,* New York and Philadelphia: Chelsea House Publishers, 1998.

www.liu.edu/cwis/library/african/movies.htm
[African Americans in Motion Pictures: The Past and Present]

http://afroamhistory.about.com/library/weekly/aa1008a.htm
[A Look Back at Minstrelsey]

http://classicfilm.about.com/library/weekly/aa020302a.htm
[The Black Experience in Hollywood]

www.africana.com/articles/H136.htm
[Films, Blacks in America]

www.ferris.edu/news/jimcrow/who.htm
[Who was Jim Crow?]

www.yaaams.org/blackimage.shtml
[Young African Americans against Media Stereotypes]

Cookie Lommel started her career as a journalist in the entertainment industry. She has interviewed hundreds of film, television and music personalities as an on-camera reporter for CNN. Her other books include biographies on the lives of Madame C. J. Walker, Robert Church, Johnnie L. Cochran Jr., Beck and Arthur Miller. Additionally, she has written *The History of Rap Music, Black Filmmakers* and a children's book about James Oglethorpe for Chelsea House.